The Law of War and Dubious Weapons

SIPRI

Stockholm International Peace Research Institute

Almqvist & Wiksell
International
Stockholm, Sweden

First published by the Stockholm International Peace Research Institute
in collaboration with
Almqvist & Wiksell International
26 Gamla Brogatan, S-111 20 Stockholm, Sweden

ISBN 91-85114-31-6

Printed in Sweden by
Tryckindustri AB, Solna 1976

PREFACE

Many SIPRI publications have described the impact of technology on armaments, drawing attention to the disastrous influence of technology on military strategies and military postures. In fact, technology appears to be one of the dominant factors in the arms race.

The tendency to use militarily all available means of destruction shows that in this field as in many others, man is increasingly the slave of technology rather than its master. And attempts to counteract this tendency by agreements on freezing armaments, or on disarmament have had very limited results.

But another approach to constrain and mitigate the use of force concerns the rules governing not the manufacture and possession of arms, but their use. From the beginning, the Red Cross – in which the International Committee of the Red Cross (ICRC) and affiliated national societies (Red Crescent, Red Lion and Sim) cooperate – has been active in this field. Initially its object was to alleviate the suffering of those who had become the victims of war. Later on, it extended its interest to an examination of the means and methods of warfare which lead to such suffering, and attempts were made to adopt laws of warfare which would restrict such means and methods.

In the past decade the ICRC has intensified its struggle for the strengthening and further development of the humanitarian laws of warfare. It felt the need for a reaffirmation of the traditional principles because of the emergence of the concept of total warfare. But it also recognized that a progressive development of the laws of war was vital, in view of the military impact of technology and of changing social and political realities. It not only took up questions of the protection of victims, but also supported initiatives limiting the use of certain weapons. It succeeded in organizing, with the support of the United Nations, the "Diplomatic Conference on the Reaffirmation and Development of International Humanitarian Law applicable in Armed Conflicts", two sessions of which were held, in 1974 and 1975. The third session is planned for 1976. This Diplomatic Conference has before it two "Draft Additional Protocols to the Geneva Conventions of August 12, 1949". In the first Protocol the ICRC has formulated proposals relating to the protection of victims of international armed conflicts. The second Protocol deals with the protection of victims of non-international armed conflicts.

One of the topics in the Protocols concerns the means of combat – the question of whether or not new weapons are in conformity with the principles of the laws of warfare. Technology has produced numerous new weapons, including weapons of mass destruction, and recent armed conflicts have shown the devastating effects of some of them. This strengthened the conviction that governments should honour the pledge expressed in the St Petersburg Declaration of 1868, in which it was suggested that new scientific improvements in arms should lead to negotiations and to understanding in order "to conciliate the necessities of war with the laws of humanity".

In the Draft Protocols, the ICRC proposed general principles concerning weapons, to be applied by the High Contracting Parties. The Diplomatic Conference decided, at Committee level, not only to formulate these principles, but also to discuss specific weapons which might be considered to be "dubious weapons", and to determine whether their use, totally or partially, should be prohibited. It decided to concentrate its discussions on specific conventional weapons, and to omit specific weapons of mass destruction, such as nuclear or biological weapons.

In view of these developments, an attempt is made here to answer the question: What are the legal principles to be applied with respect to "dubious weapons"? The answer is important for the Third Session of the Diplomatic Conference to be held in the spring of 1976. But apart from that, it is important to re-examine the present state of the law of armed conflict with respect to the means of combat, because every state has the obligation to determine whether the employment of a specific weapon would, under some or all circumstances, be prohibited by the international law of armed conflict. For this reason, the legality or illegality of the use of new conventional, as well as of non-conventional weapons is discussed in this book.

In Chapter 1 three questions concerning the legality of the use in war of "dubious weapons" are considered: Are the traditional principles of the law of war still valid? Should the progressive development of the laws of war be based on the recognition and inclusion of new principles? Does the application of the principles of the laws of war to certain new types of weapons – nuclear, chemical and biological and incendiary weapons, fragmentation weapons, small-calibre high-velocity bullets and so on – lead to the conclusion that all use of these weapons or any specific use of these weapons is illegal?

After examining the traditional principles, the conclusions are reached that the relevant principles underlying the rules of traditional international law concerning the means of combat can be summarized as follows: (a) the prohibition of superfluous injury, (b) respect for civilians, (c) the principle that the demands of humanity may prevail over the demands of warfare, and (d) the principle that the demands of peace (including cease-fires and armistices) may prevail over the demands of warfare (prohibition of treachery).

Three factors, all linked with the great changes induced by industrialization and technological weapon development, are mainly responsible for the attitude that the traditional distinction between civilians and members of the armed forces has ceased to have any great significance and that the civilian population may be made the legitimate object of military attack: (a) the growing importance of armaments and the arms industry, (b) the development of the doctrine of deterrence, and (c) the concept of "coercive warfare".

After examining the traditional principles and stressing the need for their re-affirmation, the question is considered of whether – in view of technological developments in weaponry – new principles with respect to the laws of war concerning the prohibition of specific weapons should be added to the traditional ones, and it is concluded that they should be clearly and expressly recognized. It is suggested, however, that these new principles are in essence only the consequence of principles already applied in the traditional rules of warfare.

Chapter 2 examines the application of the principles of the law of war to new, "dubious weapons": nuclear, biological and chemical, incendiary, small-calibre high-velocity and fragmentation and delayed-action weapons (including booby traps). Although the ICRC Diplomatic Conference does not deal with the first three categories a short analysis of the legal position of all seven categories is given.

The book concludes that, although during the discussions at the Diplomatic Conference it appeared that widely divergent views existed concerning the effects of specific weapons, and that in military circles there exists a certain reluctance to accept a prohibition with respect to the use of specific weapons or to specific use of weapons, mankind should not be made the slave of technology and should put a stop to the development of increasingly sophisticated means of destruction. It is also concluded that the most crucial task of the law of armed conflicts will be to prohibit in the near future, before it is too late, the use of weapons of mass destruction, especially nuclear weapons.

This book was written by Professor Bert V.A. Röling, a member of the SIPRI Governing Board, and Dr Olga Šuković, a member of the SIPRI research staff. An early draft was discussed in January 1975 in Stockholm by a group of eminent international lawyers,* whose comments SIPRI gratefully acknowledges.

January 1976   *Frank Barnaby*
                                                                             Director

* Professor G. Abi-Saab, Egypt
  Professor D. Bindschedler-Robert, Switzerland
  Dr H. Blix, Sweden
  Dr I. Brownlie, UK
  Professor E. Castrén, Finland
  Professor A. Poltorak, USSR
  Professor M. Šahović, Yugoslavia
  Professor T. Taylor, USA

CONTENTS

Chapter 1. The principles of the law of war[1]

1. *Introduction*

The International Committee of the Red Cross (ICRC) Conference of Government Experts on weapons that may cause unnecessary suffering or have indiscriminate effects was held in Geneva in 1973. The report of this Conference (ICRC, 1973a) invited governments to take international action with the aim of restraining, or even prohibiting, the use of specific kinds of new weapons which may be inhumane or indiscriminate in their effects (for example, small-calibre high-velocity bullets, incendiary weapons and fragmentation weapons). The experts in fact advised the governments to implement the decision made at St Petersburg in 1868, by which they reserved to themselves the right, whenever it was clear that scientific developments were leading towards improvement in armaments, "to come to an understanding . . . in order to maintain the principles which they have established, and to conciliate the necessities of war with the laws of humanity".

Before approaching the question of the contents of the present international law of armed combat, the relationship should be discussed between the prohibition of the use of force, as formulated in Article 2, paragraph 4 of the Charter of the United Nations, and the prohibition of the use of specific weapons.

In situations in which the use of force is forbidden, it follows that any use of any weapon is prohibited. But in cases in which the law of nations does not prohibit the use of armed force, as for example in the case of self-defence against an armed attack according to Article 51 of the UN Charter, not every weapon may be used and not all methods of combat are allowed. The right of the defender to adopt means of injuring the attacker is not unlimited. He would not be allowed, for example, to use biological weapons, because their use is prohibited in every case of armed combat.

The question arises as to whether every soldier who uses weapons in an illegal war, that is, in a war of aggression, is committing an act prohibited by international law, for which he could consequently be punished as a war criminal. Present international law does not hold the individual combatant responsible for such an act. The policy-makers who initiate and wage such a war of aggression commit the crime against peace. The combatant in such a war is not regarded as committing the crime against peace, according to the principles established in post-war trials. He is only responsible for acts in violation of the laws of war.

In his famous book *De jure belli ac pacis,* Hugo Grotius made a distinction

[1] For further reference to the legal sources, conventions, manuals, judgements and authors, see United Nations (1973).

between the law of war – the rules of international law pertaining in times of war – and the law of peace – the rules of international law pertaining in times of peace. The *jus ad bellum,* that is, the law which governs whether a state or a people may go to war, belongs to the law of peace. The *jus in bello,* the law of war, regulates the relations of the parties when war has broken out. To this law of war belong the provisions which prohibit specific weapons.

The tendency exists sometimes to confuse the prohibition of the use of force *(jus ad bellum)* and the prohibition of the use of specific weapons *(jus in bello).* One finds this tendency not only in scholarly publications, but also in statements made by government representatives at the United Nations. It may explain the wording of UN General Assembly Resolution 2936 (XXVII), adopted on 29 November 1972, in which the General Assembly declared the renunciation of the use or threat of force in all its forms and manifestations in international relations, in accordance with the Charter of the United Nations, and the permanent prohibition of the use of nuclear weapons.

Resolution 2936 (XXVII) resulted from discussions in the General Assembly, started on the initiative of the Soviet Union which had proposed as an item for the agenda "the non-use of force in international relations and permanent prohibition of the use of nuclear weapons". During the debate the Soviet delegate stated: "The essence of our proposal is that it provides for the renunciation by States of any use of force to resolve international disputes, including the use both of nuclear weapons and of such types of weapons as are commonly called conventional." (UN document A/PV. 2040, 26–33)

The representatives of Bulgaria, Czechoslovakia, Hungary, Mongolia and Poland in general supported the idea that the question of the prohibition of the use of nuclear weapons should be settled in conjunction with that of the prohibition of the use of force in international relations. The representative of Yugoslavia stated that "Yugoslavia has always pleaded in favour of the non-use of force in relations between States and the prohibition of all weapons of mass destruction, nuclear and thermonuclear in particular."

The same kind of argument was used by some opponents of General Assembly Resolution 1653 (XVI), of 24 November 1961, in which any use of nuclear weapons was declared to be a crime against mankind and civilization. Italy proposed that the issue of nuclear weapons not be made a separate prohibition, but that all use of force, including nuclear weapons, should be prohibited in the resolution, this being more in agreement with the UN Charter "which recognizes the right of countries to act in self-defense, and consequently does not exclude the use of nuclear weapons in self-defense". In the same vein, the USA argued "that article 51 of the Charter in no way imposed restrictions on the use of weapons in self-defense".

This kind of reasoning is contrary to present international law, which stipulates a general prohibition of force in international relations, but which recognizes that in special circumstances the use of force is legal, for example, the military force used in self-defence against armed attack as long as the UN

Security Council has not taken the necessary measures (Article 51 of the UN Charter); the action by air, sea or land forces taken by the Security Council (Article 42); or the joint action mentioned in Article 106. In such instances of the justified use of force, the laws of war are applicable, and consequently, "the right of belligerents to adopt means of injuring the enemy is not unlimited" (Article 22 of the Hague Regulations Respecting the Laws and Customs of War on Land, Annex to Hague Convention No. IV of 1907). The laws of armed combat govern the question of which weapons and methods of warfare are allowed, and which are forbidden. Everyone using force of arms must observe the laws of war.[2]

In the post-World War II war crime trials, aggressive and defensive actions were evidently treated as subject to the same *jus in bello*. The International Military Tribunal in Nuremberg passed no sentence on Doenitz and Raeder for unrestricted submarine warfare when it became evident that the Allies were guilty of the same offence (IMT, Nuremberg, 1946, pp. 109, 112). The purpose of the 1925 Geneva Protocol is to prohibit chemical and biological weapons in every armed combat, offensive or defensive. The prohibition of special weapons is meaningless if it applies only to the illegal use of force, in which case the use of any weapon at all is prohibited. Only if this impartiality is adopted with respect to just and unjust wars does the recognition of the existence of "laws of war", *jus in bello*, become meaningful, since both parties habitually assume that the other is the aggressor.

The present law of war

Some doubts exist as to whether the traditional general principles of humanitarian law concerning warfare are still valid today. During and since World War II, these principles have in practice often been waived or ignored, so that the important question now is whether this *de facto* use of weapons contrary to the spirit of humanitarian law has not modified or annulled these principles. For example, if the present legal position is that civilians were considered legitimate military targets (as they were in the case of the German use of V-I and V-II weapons, the mass air-strikes on German and Japanese cities, and the atomic-bomb attacks on Hiroshima and Nagasaki) and still are according to the doctrine of deterrence, or of "coercive warfare", the problem of the use of "dubious" weapons is largely academic. If "coercive warfare" – attacking civilians in order to make the war so unbearable for them that their government is forced to capitulate – is legal, it makes little sense to criticize certain weapons because they are painful and cruel.

Three questions should be answered concerning the legality of the use in war of "dubious" weapons.

The first question is: *Are the traditional principles of the law of war still valid?* According to widespread opinion, many principles of the international law of

---

[2] See further on this subject Greenspan (1959, p. 9).

armed combat were invalidated during World War II. The question is whether this is true: whether fundamental principles were abolished by the practice of the belligerents. Existing rules and principles can be eliminated by constant contrary practice. During the post-war trials of war criminals, an appeal was regularly made by the accused to the legal principle of *tu quoque:* the defence that the opposing, and now accusing, party had been guilty of the same violations of the law.[3] The editor of the *Law Reports of Trials of War Criminals* (United Nations, 1949, p. 10) came to the conclusion that: "It would thus, in strict law, be no defence for an ex-enemy to plead that a certain practice had been departed from by one or more of the Allies themselves, unless such departure were great enough to constitute evidence of a change in usage." The question of whether existing principles of the law of warfare were abolished during World War II by such "a change in usage" is a grave problem. It is a question which makes an appeal not only to reason – it is not simply an intellectual problem for which a cool analysis should provide the solution – but also to conscience. The lawyer's answer to the question, as well as being an analysis of the existing legal status, is also a contribution to the legal position, for expert opinion is a supplementary means of determining rules of international law (Statute of the International Court of Justice, Article 38, para. 1*d*). The lawyer's finding on this question is both declaratory and, to some extent, constitutive.

In determining the validity of the traditional principles, the obvious conflict between the different elements which constitute the law – the conventions, the judgements, and the customs and practices – must be taken into account. Any analysis of these conflicting elements which concludes that the humanitarian values of earlier times are no longer valid, is a factor in creating new law (and thus in contributing to invalidate old law).

Does the opinion of the experts – the lawyers – strengthen or undermine the bulwark erected against violence in the name of civilization and humanity? As a lawyer, the expert's natural tendency will be to uphold the laws of humanity against the demands of military necessity or political expediency. But as a scholar, he must carefully, and in good faith, evaluate all the evidence, both *pro* and *con*. Moreover, his opinion can have lasting influence only if he has taken all relevant social factors into account in an attempt to arrive at a legal judgement of the situation.

The second question is: *Should the progressive development of the laws of war be based on the recognition and inclusion of new principles?* The traditional principles developed partly because a conflict existed between the demands of humanity and the necessities of war.

---

[3] This defence was taken although the prosecution had, in view of the Allied practice of bombing cities, abstained from indicting the Germans, accused for attacking the civilian population (London blitz, Coventry, Rotterdam, with V-I and V-II weapons). The Court did not write out punishments for unrestricted submarine warfare (although it declared this kind of warfare illegal), because the Allies had followed the same practice. See Judgment of the IMT (1946, p. 109).

4

These values (those of humanity *vs* military necessity) were weighed against each other in point of significance, and as a result some weapons were prohibited (small explosive bullets, dum-dum bullets, and chemical and bacteriological weapons). Such prohibitions were the outcome of the application of the existing legal principles to specific weapons. Progressive development of the laws of war can be restricted to the application of these existing laws of war to new weapons, in a decision in which the demands of humanity are considered anew in relation to military effectiveness. But another question should be put and answered: Has the time come to recognize new principles of the laws of armed combat? Developments in military technology have resulted in the situation where the use of existing weapons could bring about the end of civilization, even of the whole of mankind.

This new evaluation of modern weapons – that their use can endanger mankind and its survival – has found expression in several treaties. In the Preamble to the 1967 Treaty of Tlatelolco it is stated "that nuclear weapons, whose terrible effects are suffered, indiscriminately and inexorably, by military forces and civilian population alike, constitute, through the persistence of the radioactivity they release, an attack on the integrity of the human species and ultimately may even render the whole earth uninhabitable". The Preamble to the 1968 Non-Proliferation Treaty mentions "the devastation that would be visited upon all mankind by a nuclear war". The 1971 Agreement on Measures to Reduce the Risk of Outbreak of Nuclear War between the USA and the USSR takes into account "the devastating consequences that nuclear war would have for all mankind".

Does the fact that modern warfare threatens the survival of the human race, or the survival of peoples, necessitate the adoption of new principles of the law of war? In traditional international law, the humanitarian aspect of a specific weapon may lead to its prohibition. The modern international law of warfare might include the survival aspect as a factor which may lead to the prohibition of the use of a specific weapon.

The same reasoning applies with respect to the environment. Modern technology has created the possibility of destroying the environment in which a population lives, and this destruction could be almost irreversible. Would it thus not be reasonable to include the danger for the environment (the disturbance of the ecological balance) as a factor which should lead to the prohibition of a specific weapon or to the prohibition of a specific use of a weapon (methods of warfare)? The new awareness of danger that weapons may have for the ecological balance is evidenced in resolutions of the General Assembly, and in the draft treaty proposed by the USA and the USSR for the prohibition of ecological warfare.[4]

---

[4] UN General Assembly Resolution 3246 (XXIX), 9 December 1974: "Prohibition of action to influence the environment and climate for military and other purposes incompatible with the maintenance of international security, human well-being and health". According to the Draft Convention on the Prohibition of Military or any other Hostile Use of Environmental Modification Tech-

In this respect – concerning the values of "survival" and of "environment" – the concept of the "threshold" is relevant. If recognized principles of the law of war are applied to certain modern weapons, such as nuclear weapons, there might be circumstances in which the use of such weapons would not violate these principles: one example might be the use of a small tactical nuclear weapon against a missile in outer space. Introducing nuclear weapons in this way would, however, mean crossing the "threshold" separating conventional from nuclear weapons. This crossing of the threshold would increase the probability – through escalation – of the use of other nuclear weapons and thus of general nuclear war and mutual destruction. Therefore, fear for the survival of humanity might be a factor leading to the total prohibition of a category of weapons whose use would otherwise not necessarily or in all circumstances be contrary to the principles of the laws of war. The same reasoning applies to consideration for the environment.

This threshold principle has already been applied to chemical weapons. The concept of a threshold separating conventional and chemical weapons has been a factor leading to the prohibition of all chemical weapons, including tear gases. The use of tear gases and other incapacitating chemical weapons, as such, might not be contrary to the laws of humanity. But they have been forbidden in the category of "all chemical weapons" for the reason that some use of gas might lead to general gas warfare.

Still another new development should be recognized. In the traditional law of warfare, the humanitarian aspects were evaluated against the "necessities of war". Today, however, thermonuclear weapons and certain deterrent strategies, such as the threat of counter-city attack as a second strike, are considered necessary for effective deterrence, that is, for "the maintenance of peace".

It therefore appears that a new conflict may have arisen: a conflict between the laws of humanity and the demands of peace. Must the principle that the civilian population is not a military target now be sacrificed because the threat to destroy cities – to commit a kind of genocide – can ensure the maintenance of peace?[5] Are some weapons, for instance thermonuclear weapons – notwithstanding their repulsive qualities – to continue to be recognized as legal weapons only because they are the indispensable instruments of the "balance of terror"?

Prohibition of certain new weapons

A third question should be considered: *Does the application of the principles of the laws of war* (the traditional principles, *casu quo* the adapted, modern prin-

niques, proposed to the Conference of the Committee on Disarmament (CCD) in August 1975, the parties undertake "not to engage in military or any other hostile use of environmental modification techniques having widespread, long-lasting or severe effects as a means of destruction, damage or injury to another State Party".

[5] One aim of the SALT agreements was the maintenance of a mutual second-strike capability, considering that the limitation of anti-ballistic missiles "would lead to a decrease in the risk of outbreak of war involving nuclear weapons" (preamble to the ABM Treaty).

ciples) *to certain new types of weapons* – nuclear, chemical and biological, geophysical and incendiary weapons, fragmentation weapons, small-calibre high-velocity bullets and delayed-action weapons – *lead to the conclusion that all use of these weapons, or any specific use of these weapons, is illegal?* The impact of technological developments on all weapon systems is evident: the general tendency is to incorporate into the military arsenals every new contribution to efficient weaponry. Governments and public opinion must be alerted to this creeping process of weapon sophistication.

If the use of modern weapons proves to violate the minimum "standard of humanity" as formulated in the laws of war, it should be officially prohibited. Such a prohibition might have a specific significance. While there may be some truth in the observation that the laws of war are often violated in combat as soon as such a violation serves military interests, the most important impact of a prohibition of the use of specific weapons would be felt in times of peace:[6] it would influence military posture and even military strategy. Although it would not prevent a government from wanting to acquire these weapons – laws of war are not synonymous with laws of disarmament, and forbidden weapons may be desirable for the purpose of the mutual deterrence of their use – it would be difficult for a government to rely, for defence or for general deterrence, on a weapon whose use was prohibited by law.

In general, a legal prohibition on the use of a specific weapon may contribute to the elimination of any possession of that weapon through disarmament measures, as was the case of the prohibition on the possession of biological weapons in the 1972 Biological Weapons Convention, which was preceded by a prohibition on the use of these weapons.

In the sections to follow, the question will be answered: What are the legal principles to be applied with respect to "dubious weapons"? The answer is important for the two ICRC Conferences at which the two Additional Protocols to the 1949 Geneva Conventions will be discussed (the Second Conference of Government Experts, February 1976, and the Third Session of the Diplomatic Conference, about two months later). But apart from that, it is important to reexamine the present state of the law of armed conflict. For it is the duty of every government to evaluate independently modern weapons, and to determine whether they are to be considered forbidden weapons. This duty was underlined in a new Article 34 of Protocol I adopted at the Second Session of the Diplomatic Conference:

---

[6] Compare Shakespeare's *King Henry V* (Act III, scene 3), where King Henry claimed to be powerless to keep his soldiers under control in and after battle:

"What rein can hold licentious wickedness
When down the hill he holds his fierce career?"

but to be able to enforce regulations in time of peace:

"Whiles yet my soldiers are in my command;
Whiles yet the cool and temperate wind of grace
O'erblows the filthy and contagious clouds
Of heady murder, spoil, and villany."

In the study, development, acquisition, or adoption of a new weapon, means or method of warfare, a High Contracting Party is under an obligation to determine whether its employment would, under some or all circumstances be prohibited by this Protocol or by any other rule of international law applicable to the High Contracting Party.

II. *The traditional principles of the law of war*

Unnecessary suffering

War is an exceptional state of law in which destruction and killing are permitted, although not without restrictions (see Article 22 of the 1907 Hague Regulations).

In the seventeenth century, Hugo Grotius taught that *"in bello omnia licere quae necessaria sunt ad finem belli" (De jure belli ac pacis, Book III,1. 2).* The traditional *jus in bello* only included one aspect of this principle – that is, that an act of violence which does not further the aim of the war is not permitted. This is perhaps the only undisputed rule of warfare: that acts of violence which are not necessary to the conduct of war are prohibited. But opinions differ on which acts are necessary and which are not.

If unnecessary violence is prohibited, it follows logically that violence which causes *disproportionate* suffering to soldiers or civilians compared with the military gains is also prohibited. Here, however, opinions differ, and it is clear that any principle of proportionality contains a value judgement which makes its application in times of combat very dubious, since it depends on subjective reasoning.

The principle of the prohibition of "unnecessary suffering" or "superfluous injury" finds application in the prohibition on wounding or killing soldiers who have surrendered at discretion (Article 23*c* of the 1907 Hague Regulations) and on declaring that no quarter will be given (Article 23*d*). Another more general application is the prohibition of weapons calculated to cause unnecessary suffering (Article 23*e*). Thus, for instance, if a bullet can, by hitting and disabling a soldier, eliminate him from battle, it must not be reconstructed in such a way that it inflicts unhealable wounds, or renders death inevitable.

Respect for the civilian population

Related to the principle that violence which does not further the war aim is prohibited is the general principle of the distinction between soldiers and civilians. When wars were fought by standing armies, this distinction was understandable and obvious: civilians were not involved in armed conflicts and were expected to remain passive. In fact, civilians were not permitted to participate in warfare.[7] The assumption that violence directed against civilians could not

---

[7] Except in the case of the closely defined *levée en masse* (Article 2, Hague Regulations), the special case in which civilians attained the position of privileged combatants.

further the conduct of war gave rise to the general principle, accepted in the 1868 Declaration of St Petersburg, "that the only legitimate object which States should endeavour to accomplish during war is to weaken the military forces of the enemy": that attacks on civilians as such are prohibited. Although this principle is not expressly formulated as a rule in the formal conventions, it finds expression in the prohibition on attacking undefended buildings, towns or ports (Article 25 of the Hague Regulations; Article 1, Hague Convention IX).

In the traditional law of war, however, exceptions to the general prohibitions on deliberately injuring the civilian population as such were recognized, especially in the rules of naval warfare. The blockade was not forbidden,[8] nor was the naval bombardment of towns if the local authorities declined to deliver necessary supplies to the rival forces (Article 3, Hague Convention IX). Military necessity (the need to secure supplies) provided, in this case, the authority to coerce civilians by violent means.

The prohibition on deliberately attacking the civilian population as such is not based exclusively on the principle of avoiding unnecessary suffering. Other humanitarian aspects apparently also played a role, leading to the legal obligation to take into account the interests of the civilian population. Several rules of international law concerning warfare are based on the principle that the civilian population should be spared as far as possible. The clearest example of this principle is found in the rules concerning warning before bombardment (Article 26, Hague Regulations; Article 2, Hague Convention IX).

The principle of proportionality

Another consequence of respect for civilians as a basic principle governing restrictions in warfare is the rule that acts of force against military targets must be renounced if they cause disproportionate suffering to the civilian population.

It is questionable, however, whether this principle of "proportionality" was ever expressly recognized as a definite rule of international law. Certainly Article 26 of the 1906 Hague Regulations required the officer commanding an attacking force to do all in his power to warn the authorities of the impending attack. Article 2 of Hague Convention IX also required definite warning to be given if this were at all possible, but for the rest it permitted "any unavoidable damage". However, the code for the law of air warfare, formulated in 1923, took this principle as a point of departure. Military targets were listed in detail,[9] and it was laid down that these targets should only be bombed if this could be

---

[8] Starving civilians in order to force them to demand their governments' capitulation has played a role in many wars. Article 17 of the 1863 Lieber Instructions states: "War is not carried on by arms alone. It is lawful to starve the hostile belligerent, armed or unarmed, so that it leads to the speedier subjection of the enemy."

[9] Article 24:2 of the 1923 Hague Draft Rules on Aerial Warfare included "factories constituting important and well-known centres engaged in the manufacture of arms, ammunition or distinctively military supplies".

done "without the indiscriminate bombardment of the civilian population" (Article 24:3, 1923 Hague Draft Rules on Aerial Warfare). These rules of air warfare, however, were never confirmed by treaty, and the common practice of aerial bombardment suggests that the rules have not acquired the force of custom.

Now that weapons of mass destruction have become available, the time has come to recognize that this principle of proportionality amounts to the rule that an attack on a legitimate military target is prohibited if it will cause disproportionate suffering to the civilian population.

The principle of proportionality follows logically from the principles that civilians as such may not be the target of attack and that they must be spared as much as possible. Its significance today, as a consequence of the emergence of weapons of mass destruction, makes it advisable to give more weight to this concept, and to emphasize its importance by an express formulation in the laws of war.

The principle of proportionality strengthens the respect for the civilian population. This respect in the first place, according to the traditional law of warfare, leads to a prohibition of an attack on the civilian population as such. In addition, it leads to the prohibition of an attack on a legitimate military target, if the unavoidable accidental loss of civilian life or property would be disproportionate to the military gains.

As a corollary of this rule concerning the protection of civilians, the prohibition of "blind" weapons, that is, those which cannot discriminate between combatants and non-combatants, should be recognized. If the civilian population is to be protected as far as possible, it follows that weapons with indiscriminate effects must also be prohibited.

Weapons that cause disproportionate suffering for the civilian population, or that cannot discriminate should be forbidden. But it is feasible that weapons exist, which might be used without disproportionate or indiscriminate effects, but whose employment has generally led to disproportionate suffering of the population, or to indiscriminate use. Weapons may exist, the illegal use of which is characteristic. Here again, there would be reason to prohibit all use of the weapon, although legitimate employment of the weapon is feasible. The decisive factor would be actual experience of the manner in which the weapon is usually employed.

Doubt may exist whether such a prohibition has already been recognized in the traditional law of armed conflict. But the point that this rule ought to be regarded as part of the laws of war is important, rather than the question of whether it is traditional law, or through progressive development, modern international law.

The topic is dealt with in this chapter, because it must be treated in connection with the principles related to disproportionate suffering and indiscriminate effects. The "extension" of the prohibition follows from the application of another principle: despite the fact that weapons can be used, in specific and exceptional circumstances, in a manner which is not prohibited, these same weapons should be subject to a total prohibition when the manner in which they are commonly used is in violation of the laws of war.

The laws of humanity

Although only those means which can further the aims of war may be adopted, not everything that is *ad finem belli* is permitted: principles of civilization and humanity impose their own restrictions. Hence there are limitations with respect to certain classes of persons (prisoners of war, the sick and the wounded, the shipwrecked, civilians detained by the enemy), and to certain classes of buildings (places of worship, places of learning, cultural and artistic monuments, hospitals and other charitable institutions). Hence, too, there are limitations on certain classes of weapons ("poison or poisoned weapons are banned under Article 23 of the Hague Regulations and chemical and biological weapons are banned under the 1925 Geneva Protocol).

The demands of humanity, which must be considered in determining the legality or prohibition of a specific weapon, have been formulated in three important documents. The 1868 Declaration of St Petersburg (see page 1) stipulates that governments must "conciliate the necessities of war with the laws of humanity".

Second, the demands of humanity are evaluated in the prohibition of chemical weapons in the 1925 Geneva Protocol for, although it cannot be denied that chemical weapons can be used in a militarily effective way, they are nevertheless forbidden, so the principle of unnecessary suffering was not the decisive factor.

In addition, chemical weapons can in specific circumstances be used exclusively against military targets, so the principle of indiscriminate use was not decisive.

Chemical weapons were prohibited because of their repulsive and disgusting character; that is, the humanitarian aspects were weighed against the military advantages, and the humanitarian considerations prevailed.

Third, the "de Martens clause" was inserted in the preamble to Hague Convention IV on the laws of land warfare. According to this preamble, in cases not covered by the Regulations, "the inhabitants and the belligerents remain under the protection and the rule of the principles of the law of nations, as they result from the usages established among civilized peoples, from the laws of humanity, and the dictates of the public conscience". Here, although direct reference is made to the principles of the law of nations, the laws of humanity and the demands of the public conscience are expressly mentioned, which implies that they are legally significant each time existing principles of the law of warfare are interpreted and the adoption or recognition of new principles of international law is considered. In this context it is noteworthy that the de Martens clause was expressly recognized again in 1949. Parties to the Geneva Conventions of 1949 were reminded of the fact that in case of renunciation of the Hague Conventions, they were to remain bound by the rule expressed in the de Martens clause.[10]

In its Draft Additional Protocol of 1973, the ICRC proposed a more clearly expressed formulation of the principle that the demands of humanity play a role with respect to the contents of the law of warfare. In the preamble it is stated: "Recalling that, in cases not covered by conventional or customary international law, the civilian population and the combatants remain under the protection of the principles of humanity and the dictates of the public conscience" (ICRC, 1973b).

The Diplomatic Conference adopted, at the Committee level, a revised version of the de Martens clause. Article 1:4 of Draft Protocol I reads:

In cases not included in the present Protocol or in any other instrument of treaty law, civilians and combatants remain under the protection and authority of the principles of international law derived from established custom, from the principles of humanity and from the dictates of public conscience (UN, 1975, Annex I, p. 2).

It is clear that the demands of humanity will often conflict with the demands of warfare or the "necessities of war". Until now, specific prohibitions based on the "laws of humanity and the dictates of the public conscience" have been recognized only where the military advantages did not weigh heavily. Thus chemical and biological weapons are forbidden, but no express prohibition exists with respect to nuclear weapons.[11]

The necessities of war

Opinions differ on the theory of military necessity. In his important book on the laws of armed conflict, Schwarzenberger (1968, p. 12) classifies the provision of war into three types, according to how they interact with military necessity: (a) rules which limit acts of war unconditionally, in which the standards of civilization take precedence and no appeals to military necessity are allowed; (b) rules which remove the limitation on acts of war in cases of necessity, that is, where there is a real compromise between the standards of civilization and military necessity; and (c) rules which recognize the supremacy of military necessity.

The history of military necessity as a factor which can override rules of warfare is not quite clear. The preamble to Hague Convention IV of 1907 states:

[10] See Article 63, Convention I of the 1949 Geneva Conventions; Article 62, Convention II; Article 142, Convention III; and Article 158, Convention IV.

[11] Liddell Hart (1960, p. 62) considers it absurd to prohibit chemical weapons "while adopting the use of nuclear weapons – which are weapons of mass-slaughter, and violate the lawful code of warfare on more counts than such a weapon as mustard gas, which is relatively humane". It should be stressed here that the favourable evaluation of chemical weapons by Liddell Hart and others – for example, Fuller (1961, p. 174) – does not take into account the discoveries in chemical weapons since World War I.

According to the views of the High Contracting Parties, these provisions, the wording of which has been inspired by the desire to diminish the evils of war, as far as military requirements permit, are intended to serve as a general rule of conduct for the belligerents in their mutual relations and in their relations with the inhabitants.

Since "military requirements" are referred to here in general terms, the concern is with a broader definition than the "principle of self-preservation". The latter is only operative if the existence of the state itself is at stake, and cannot be invoked by military expedience or even military necessity in a particular action. Those who are inclined to give decisive emphasis to military necessity differ about which military values may be considered to be of overriding interest. Hence, concerning the standpoint that *Kriegsräson geht vor Kriegsmanier,* Julius Stone has declared: "The general point of criticism of the German doctrine is undoubtedly the extended notion of 'necessity' held thus to justify the overriding of the law of war, a notion covering not merely the needs of military survival, but also lesser dangers, and even the needs of positive military success" (Stone, 1959, p. 352).

The commas separating the words "as far as military requirements permit" from the preceding and immediately following words (see above) are important. Does the preamble refer to a general limitation, which can therefore still be invoked? Or was there a wish to state that, in the rules as laid down, military necessity had already continually been taken into account? In other words: do the words "as far as military requirements permit" refer to "the desire to diminish the evils of war" (such that this desire would have taken into account those military requirements), or do they refer to "these provisions. . . are intended to serve as a general rule of conduct for the belligerents" (such that these provisions are only a rule of conduct as far as military requirements permit)?

At the 1899 deliberations at the Hague, the German delegate proposed the generally restricting clause *"pour autant que les nécessités militaires le permettent"*. This proposal was rejected, but a report by Rolin was approved in which the following paragraph appeared: *"Au surplus, comme le Colonel de Gross de Schwarzhoff l'a fait observer sans soulever de contradiction, ces restrictions ne sauraient entraver la liberté d'action des belligérants dans certaines éventualités extrêmes qu'on peut assimiler à une sorte de légitime défense."*[12]

Does this in fact mean *Kriegsräson geht vor Kriegsmanier?* The Netherlands Special Court of Cessation, in the case against Rauter (12 January 1949, *Nederlandse Jurisprudentie 1949,* No. 87) expressly denied this, on the grounds that some provisions of the Hague Regulations explicitly provide exceptions for military necessity. The judgement given by a US tribunal against Field Marshal List stated: "The rules of international law must be followed even if it results in the loss of a battle or even a war" *(Trials of War Criminals,* Vol.

---

[12] For further discussion, and for the references, see Röling's lectures before the Hague Academy on the application of the laws of war in the post-war judgements (Röling, 1961, pp. 329–456, 385 ff.).

XI, p. 1277).[13] This, then, is the jurists' opinion. Military practice did not agree: belligerents most often inflicted any kind of damage considered necessary, or even only useful, for the conduct of war.

From the fact that some provisions in the 1907 Hague Regulations explicitly provide exceptions for the case of necessity (for example, Article 23g, Hague Convention V), the conclusion can be drawn that these rules have already taken into account the military necessity. Such a military necessity, consequently, can no longer justify acts which are forbidden in the Regulations. It is quite another question for a judge to take into account the special circumstance of military necessity in determining the punishment.

The demands of peace

Apart from limitations based on the principles of civilization and humanity, the origin of some limitations of warfare can be traced back to a prohibition which Kant formulated as *"sich solcher heimtückischen Mittel zu bedienen, die das Vertrauen, welches zu künftiger Gründung eines dauerhaften Friedens erforderlich ist, vernichten würden" (Die Metaphysik der Sitten,* 1797, para. 57). This principle was adopted by the 1863 Lieber Instructions: Article 16 states that the military necessity "admits of deception, but disclaims acts of perfidy; and, in general, military necessity does not include any act of hostility which makes the return to peace unnecessarily difficult".

It is prohibited, then, to perform actions which exclude or obstruct the chances of re-establishing peaceful relations. While the vagueness of this criterion makes it virtually unfit for direct application, its significance lies in the fact that it has led to the formulation of specific concrete limitations on the use of force. It underlies such limitations as the prohibition "to kill or wound treacherously individuals belonging to the hostile nation or army" (Article 23b, Hague Regulations), or to misuse the white flag of truce or the uniform of the enemy (Article 23f).

It is, of course, difficult to make a clear distinction between legitimate "ruses of war" and forbidden acts of treachery. The decisive criterion is given by the International Committee of the Red Cross in Article 35, Protocol I and Article 21, Protocol II: acts of perfidy are defined as "acts inviting the confidence of the adversary with intent to betray that confidence (ICRC, 1972).[14]

It should be noted that this principle of restriction of violence is based not on considerations concerning "the necessities of war" but on those of "the

---

[13] Compare also the judgement against Krupp (UN, 1949, Vol. IX, p. 1347) and von Leeb (*Trials of War Criminals,* Vol. XI, p. 541).

[14] Another application of the concept of perfidy was suggested at the Conference of Government Experts in Lucerne, 1974: the use of any weapon in such a way that it places the intended victim under a moral, juridical or humanitarian obligation to act in such a way as to endanger his safety (ICRC, 1975, para 251). Reference was made in this connection to booby traps fixed to dead bodies or to wounded soldiers.

necessities of peace". The prohibitions aim at preventing acts which might diminish the chances for a cease-fire and the conclusion of peace.

Conclusions

The relevant principles underlying the rules of traditional international law can be summarized as follows:
1. The prohibition of superfluous injury, hence
    (*a*) the prohibition of weapons which cause unnecessary suffering,
    (*b*) the prohibition of weapons which cause disproportionate suffering.
2. The distinction between civilians and soldiers, hence
    (*a*) the prohibition of an attack on civilians as such,
    (*b*) the duty to spare the civilian population as much as possible,
    (*c*) the prohibition of military acts which cause disproportionate suffering of civilians,
    (*d*) the prohibition of "blind" or indiscriminate weapons,
    (*e*) the prohibition of weapons that are usually employed in such a manner that they cause disproportionate suffering or have indiscriminate effects.[15]
3. The principle that the demands of humanity may prevail over the demands of warfare.
4. The principle that the demands of the conclusions of peace (including cease-fire and armistice) may prevail over the demands of warfare (prohibition of treachery).   .

III. *Consideration of the impact of modern warfare*

In recent years, the traditional distinction between civilians and members of the armed forces has been eroded; indeed, it is now felt in many circles that this distinction has ceased to have any great significance and that the civilian population may be made the legitimate object of military attack. Consequently it is felt that, because the suffering of the civilian population has become an objective of military activity, it is nonsense to discuss "weapons that cause unnecessary suffering". Three factors, all linked with the great changes induced by industrialization and technological developments in weaponry, are mainly responsible for this change of attitude: (*a*) the growing importance of armaments and the arms industry; (*b*) the development of the doctrine of deterrence; and (*c*) the concept of "coercive warfare".

---

[15] It might be argued that this principle does not belong to the traditional law of warfare, but rather to its progressive development. The dividing line is difficult to draw. The crucial point is that this principle should be recognized as a criterion to evaluate modern weapons.

The influence of armaments and the arms industry

The *jus in bello,* as we know it, developed from customary law which in turn arose from wars conducted between relatively small professional armies. But industrial and technological developments have attached increasing importance to armaments; war has become a matter of "manned arms" rather than of "armed men" and victory or defeat has become increasingly dependent on the capacity of the armaments industries. Moreover, technological developments in weaponry – long-range artillery, aircraft and missiles – have made armaments industries and their transportation systems new targets of attack. So the status of civilians working in such industries has become an important issue: Can they continue to enjoy the protection that they were formerly granted as civilians?

Because the effectiveness of the armaments industry has become of decisive importance for the outcome of a war, it is no longer true that civilians take no part in the business of war. A tendency has consequently arisen to deny workers in munitions industries their protected status, and to regard them instead as "quasi-combatants". Armaments factories and naval dockyards have always been considered legitimate targets. But are these targets to be limited to buildings and machinery or may they also include the personnel?

The exceptional legal status of workers in war industries was recognized in Article 2 of the Draft Agreement relating to Hospital and Safety Zones and Localities: "No persons residing, in whatever capacity, in a hospital and safety zone shall perform any work, either within or without the zone, directly connected with military operations or the production of war material".[16] This suggests that workers in war industries should not be allowed to secure their own safety by withdrawing to the safety zones after working hours.

Article 4c of the Draft Agreement states that these safety zones "shall be far removed and free from all military objectives, or large industrial or administrative establishments". The 1954 Hague Convention for the Protection of Cultural Property in the Event of Armed Conflict contained a non-restrictive summary of "any important military objective constituting a vulnerable point, such as, for example, an aerodrome, broadcasting station, establishment engaged upon work of national defence, a port or railway station of relative importance or a main line of communication".

With the increasing importance of armaments and arms industries as decisive factors in war, it cannot be maintained that an attack on personnel working in the arms industry – sometimes highly skilled personnel who cannot easily be replaced – would not serve any military purpose. For instance, the elimination of nuclear- or ballistic-weapon scientists could have considerable impact on the military power of the opponent, even on the outcome of the war.

---

[16] This Draft Agreement is contained in Annex I to Geneva Convention IV relative to the Protection of Civilian Persons in Time of War of August 12, 1949.

Arguments for sparing workers in these industries have therefore become weak. Consequently, practices of warfare have changed. The weaponry of World War I could not be used for attacking workers in the arms industries so that, although the army had become *la nation en armes,* limited technology saved the home front from major attack: *"Seule l'inefficacité des moyens techniques assura à cette époque l'immunité des arrières"* (Wanty, 1968, pp. 256 – 66). But in World War II, arms factories as well as workers' homes became targets for aerial bombardment.

The danger exists that the practice of World War II might be repeated in any future war. But if workers in armament factories are considered lawful military targets, then the immunity of the civilian population is brought into question, for it is not possible to distinguish among categories of civilians.

Consequently one must be very careful with this concept of "quasi-combatants". They have obtained, as we saw, a special, less protected status in the proposed regulation concerning the safety zones. But modern law of war refuses to consider those quasi-combatants as legitimate military targets. The ICRC Diplomatic Conference adopted a definition of the "civilian population" without excluding workers in armament industries.

The influence of the strategy of deterrence

The development of nuclear weapons and missiles has brought about an important change in the function of military power. At one time, the objective of military power was simply to achieve victory. Although dominance is still an objective in relations between the great powers and the small states, in their sphere of influence or outside that sphere, or among small powers (for example, the conflict between Israel and the Arab countries),[17] this objective has almost disappeared in relations among the great powers. If NATO and the Warsaw Treaty Organization (WTO) were to wage all-out war, the question of victory would have little meaning since such a conflict would result in mutual destruction before the issue of who was the stronger could be settled.[18]

Nor does the possession of nuclear weapons enable a country to protect its own citizens from the weapons of an enemy. Both the United States and the Soviet Union possess a far greater potential for destruction than any state has ever possessed before, but if total war broke out, there would be nothing to prevent them from reducing each other to rubble. The city walls of earlier times offered better protection to citizens than do today's defensive forces.

---

[17] Karl Deutsch (1973, p. 20) wrote that war has become the privilege of the weak and underdeveloped states.

[18] McNamara, then US Secretary of Defense, stated in a speech in San Francisco on 17 September 1967 that "the blunt unescapable fact remains that the Soviet Union could still – with its present forces – effectively destroy the United States, even after absorbing the full weight of an American first strike" (*Survival,* 1967, pp. 342–46).

The function of nuclear weapons has therefore been focussed mainly on "deterrence", that is, preventing war by threatening to use these weapons. This is the old idea of *si vis pacem para bellum*, in which the "balance of power" has been supplemented by the "balance of terror". Because of the certainty that the mutual use of nuclear weapons would bring terrible destruction to both sides, it has become of paramount importance to both countries to avoid war between themselves. The certainty that this destruction would be mutual is assured by the fact that both countries have the capacity to inflict intolerable damage with invulnerable "second-strike" weapons after the enemy's full-scale attack has been absorbed. It is a system of "mutual assured destruction".

To gain the maximum deterrent effect, it is considered necessary to hold out the prospect of using nuclear weapons against cities. According to the prevailing theory, there can only be reliable deterrence if there is a mutually assured destruction of population centres through an invulnerable second-strike capacity.[19] As General André Beaufre approvingly declared: *"La logique propre à la dissuasion impose donc de proclamer possible le génocide qui, par ailleurs, on se flatte d'empêcher."* Because Beaufre believes that deterrence will succeed in preventing war, he warns against eliminating these threats to cities by legal prohibition, arms control or disarmament. He considers it desirable *"que l'on ne réduise pas son influence pacifiante par un maniement erroné des accords de contrôle et de désarmament"*. According to him, it is simply *"le paradoxe d'une guerre non pas humanisée, mais empêchée par son horreur, proclamée et reconnue"* (*Colloque sur l'Etat moderne,* 1968, p. 21).

The nightmare of the deterrence strategist is the "disarming first-strike capability" – against his own strategic force. If both parties have such a disarming first-strike capability, the principle of deterrence breaks down. In times of crisis such a situation would be disastrous; the side which started the war would be the victor; therefore the decisive motive for taking the initiative would be the fear that the other side would attack first.

Because technological developments could not guarantee the maintenance of a second-strike capability, the great powers agreed – in the SALT agreements of 1972 – to postpone the possibility of a disarming first strike. By limiting ABM systems in each country to two in 1972, and to one (of 100 missiles) in 1974, the cities of both countries were kept open for destruction, that is, the populations of both countries were kept in the position of hostages for the good, that is, non-aggressive, conduct of their governments. This means that the hostage system has been enlarged, one might say democratized. In former

---

[19] Morton Deutsch (1961, pp. 57–68) lists mutual civilian vulnerability as one of the eight conditions under which deterrence can succeed. His argument is intended as a warning that the demands of weapon superiority conflict with the concept of stable deterrence, since the chances of war are increased by the provocative effects of such demands. "We must recognize that just as military inferiority is dangerous, so is military superiority, we neither want to tempt nor to frighten a potential enemy into military action" (*ibid.,* p. 59).

centuries the children of the kings were made hostages; nowadays it is the children of the big cities.[20]

This poses a serious problem for the lawyer. If deterrence, through the mutual threat of destruction of the civilian population, would guarantee the maintenance of peace, it would be difficult to reject this method on ethical or humanitarian grounds. *Primum vivere, deinde philosophari* would have validity, also in our time.

But deterrence does not guarantee the maintenance of peace. In his famous speech in the House of Commons on 1 March 1955, Churchill called safety "the sturdy child of terror", and survival aimed at through deterrence "the twin brother of annihilation". The balance of terror is a dangerous way of keeping the peace. One may even go further and maintain that peacekeeping by the balance of terror will inevitably lead to disaster.

In the micropolitical relationship between two powers or two alliances, the philosophy of deterrence is reasonable and logical. In the modern world every state must provide for its own security, since no world authority capable of guaranteeing security exists. Powerlessness in such a world may invite the misbehaviour of a neighbour, and so some power, including military power, is needed. Armaments are indispensable. They are the price to be paid for national sovereignty.

Armaments have a logic of their own, however, in that they tend to produce arms races (stimulated by continuous technological advances) leading to a gigantic overkill. The more or less invisible impact of the "military-industrial complex" repeatedly leads to rearmament for other than security reasons. But the main factor in the constant extension of military power – and thus of arms races – is the philosophy of maximum deterrence: the doctrine that deterrence is only effective if a country is stronger, so that it could expect to be victorious in case of war. Such a philosophy is a constant factor of anxiety and mistrust, and it causes, and constantly feeds, arms races.

Analysis of the present world situation leads to the conclusion that the earth is becoming an ever more dangerous place in which to live: the spread of nuclear weapons cannot be prevented, the NPT notwithstanding (SIPRI, 1972*b*; SIPRI, 1974*b*), and the major arms race between the great powers is accompanied by local arms races all over the world. In his impressive book *Kriegsfolgen und Kriegsverhütung,* von Weizsäcker (1971) comes to the conclusion that the result of a future war in Europe will be disastrous, and that we are on the road to that disaster.

Where great-power confrontation is most direct, there is little danger of deliberate war, that is, of war in the sense described by von Clausewitz as a means of national policy. In any case it is in preventing this kind of war that the policy

---

[20] It should be noted that Article 34 of the Red Cross Convention of 1949 relating to the protection of civilian persons in time of war, prohibits "the taking of hostages". But Article 34 concerns "protected persons", and civilians are only protected persons if they find themselves "in the hands of a Party . . . of which they are not nationals".

of maximum deterrence may be effective. Given the destructive power of modern weapons, it would be illogical for the highly developed nations to continue to use war as a deliberate means of national policy. But another kind of war is more likely – an unintentional, accidental war, an unpremeditated war brought about by miscalculation or by a crisis which has got out of hand. The possibility of this kind of war is enhanced by deterrence and the consequent arms race, overkill and the widespread presence of weapons of mass destruction.

The concept of peace through deterrence, which on a micropolitical level may be logical and reasonable, develops through the theory and practice of maximum deterrence into a deadly logic – a logic of madness. On the macropolitical scale it produces a world in which nuclear disaster is almost inevitable.

Another observation might be relevant. With respect to nuclear weapons, the application of the deterrence theory underwent some changes. The SALT agreements aim at preventing a disarming first-strike capability and maintaining the balance of terror by, mutually, keeping the big cities open for destruction. But by doing so, the use of the thermonuclear strategic weapons has lost its credibility, except in the worst case that the opponent starts to use them. The function of strategic weapons then becomes the deterrence of the use of these weapons rather than the deterrence of war. If strategic weapons – through the absence of effective ABM systems – mutually guarantee the deaths of millions of people, it would not be reasonable to employ them, and therefore they will not be used in a conventional war. Such use would be sheer madness. The threat is therefore no longer credible, as long as statesmen and military commanders act rationally. Of course, strategic weapons may be used out of despair, hatred or stupidity, and therefore some element of deterrence derives from the sheer existence of these weapons. But their real function has become to deter the use of the thermonuclear strategic weapons of the opponent, and no longer to deter war.

In Europe, the conviction is growing that the use of tactical nuclear weapons would mean the destruction of Europe. Unfortunately, in many political and military circles the opinion prevails that NATO conventional forces are not strong enough to deter attack; that therefore tactical nuclear weapons are indispensable for deterrence; and that consequently all options to employ, if necessary, tactical nuclear weapons should be left open.[21] But opinion is gradually changing. More and more experts declare that the NATO conventional forces are strong enough to deter, and in case of failure of deterrence, to withstand the opposing conventional forces. The conviction increasingly grows that the weapon posture in Europe is too dangerous, since Europe would be totally destroyed in a future war. Consequently, in Europe too, opinion emerges which would restrict the function of tactical nuclear weapons to the deterrence of the use of these weapons by the opponent. In this view the deterrence function of

---

[21] See, for instance, the Atlantic Declaration of 19 June 1974.

tactical nuclear weapons would change: from deterring war to mutually deterring the use of tactical weapons. Some experts have already realized "that the most you can do with the nuclear weapons is simply to negate the nuclear weapons on the other side, and that it is very difficult to translate nuclear weapons into political gains simply because the scale of destructiveness is disproportionate to any political objective" (Shulman, 1971, p. 264).

For all these reasons, the arguments that "deterrence through mutual assured destruction serves the cause of peace", that "the balance of terror is needed to prevent war" or that "deterrence, including counter-city strategy, is a necessary condition for peace" carry no conviction. They should be rejected on practical grounds.

Whatever the legal position of nuclear weapons as such may be, it is wrong to suppose that we must abandon the principle of the law of war that "attack of the civilian population as such is prohibited", simply because deterrence in the name of peace demands it.

This critique of "deterrence" concerns the maximum-deterrence theory as adopted and practised by the parties in the Cold War. Proponents of the theory of maximum deterrence strive, as a minimum, for parity, evaluating their own power very conservatively, and attributing excessive qualities to the arms of the opponent. Military power should, in this view, be able to deter, and if deterrence fails, to win the war. This philosophy leads inevitably to an arms race and to almost unlimited overkill. For this reason the conviction grew "that criteria for effective deterrence could prove quite different from criteria for fighting and winning".[22]

A deterrence theory in which weapons would only serve to deter the use of weapons by the opponent by making attack unattractive for the opponent – the theory of minimum deterrence – would exclude this feature of stimulating fear, uncertainty and military strength. In the theory of "defensive deterrence" – where the arms are focussed on defence against attack, and as far as possible are not suitable for offensive purposes – the military posture might be the precondition for de-escalation in armaments. The prohibition of the use of nuclear weapons except as reprisal in kind in response to the use of nuclear weapons by the opponent (that is, the exclusion of nuclear blackmail) fits this military posture.

In addition, and in view of this, the time has come to reconsider the legal position of nuclear weapons. If it is time to reduce their function from deterring war to primarily deterring the use of these weapons, the demands of peace are no longer an obstacle to outlawing these weapons. The legal prohibition of the use of nuclear weapons would perfectly reflect their actual position and function between nuclear powers. No considerations of the necessities of war or the demands of peace are obstacles for such a general prohibition of the use of weapons which cannot but have indiscriminate effects, and which are repul-

---

[22] Compare Thomas W. Milburn, in Pruitt and Snyder (1969, p. 264).

sive weapons threatening the integer existence of the human environment, if not of humanity itself.

One of the primordial aims of the laws of war should be to outlaw nuclear weapons.

The concept of coercive warfare

A third factor which has led to civilian populations becoming targets in war is the strategy of coercive warfare, that is, a strategy whereby civilians are attacked in order to make the war so unbearable for them that their government is forced to capitulate. The idea of this kind of warfare is not new; it was practised in ancient Greece. And, as mentioned above, Article 17 of the 1863 Lieber Instructions expressly states that "it is lawful to starve the hostile belligerent, armed or unarmed so that it leads to speedier subjection of the enemy".

The practice of coercive warfare went much further than this in the American Civil War. General Sherman, who devastated Atlanta and terrorized the rest of Georgia and was called the Attila of the American Continent (Fuller, 1961, pp. 108 ff.), operated on the principle that "The only possible way to end this unhappy and dreadful conflict. . . is to make it terrible beyond endurance." General Sheridan accepted the same premise in the war against the American Indians.

This concept of warfare against civilians remained latent in the limited wars waged in nineteenth-century Europe. Even in World War I, Russia threatened and indeed carried out its threat to try pilots who bombed undefended cities (Mouton, 1957, p. 443). The 1919 Commission on Responsibilities of the War and on Enforcement of Penalties included the "deliberate bombardment of undefended places" in its list of war crimes. But in World War II the practice of attacking cities and population centres was revived. A contributing factor was the development of air power which made possible attacks on civilian populations far behind the front lines. Indeed, World War II exhibited a form of warfare in which the heaviest explosives were dropped on large cities, for example, in the London blitz, in the bombing of German cities culminating in the destruction of Dresden,[23] and the systematic fire-bombing of Japanese cities (in which sometimes more than 80 000 inhabitants were burned to death in one night) culminating in the atomic-bomb attacks on Hiroshima and Nagasaki – two of the five cities which had been spared so as to destroy them in an exemplary fashion. World War II thus saw the introduction of the concept of strategic bombing to make the war "painful beyond endurance". Referring

---

[23] Significant here was the "Casablanca directive" issued by the British and US bomber commands in the UK on 4 February 1943: "Your primary object will be the progressive destruction and dislocation of the German military, industrial, and economic system, and the undermining of the morale of the German people to a point where their capacity for armed resistance is fatally weakened" (Churchill, 1952, p. 458).

to the use of the atomic bomb against Japan, Schelling (1966, p. 17) states: "The two bombs were in the tradition of Sheridan against the Comanches and Sherman in Georgia. These were weapons of terror and shock. The political target of the bomb was not the dead of Hiroshima or the factories they worked in, but the survivors in Tokyo."

The war in Viet-Nam followed the same pattern. The bombing of North Viet-Nam was "the direct exercise of the power to hurt" (*ibid.*, p. 196). The Viet-Nam War demonstrated "the kind of continuous coercive warfare that was introduced by the bombing of North Vietnam in February 1965". That bombing "was an effort to raise the costs of warfare to North Vietnam and to make them readier to come to terms" (*ibid.*, p. 170).[24] So it is easy to understand why Schelling contends that: "In the present era non-combatants appear to be not only deliberate targets but primary targets" (*ibid.*, p. 27). That is the lesson of World War II and the practice of the leading nations today.

Soviet theory takes the same line, although expressed less forcefully than in US strategic writings. In his authoritative book *Soviet Military Strategy* Marshal V.D. Sokolovskiy of the Soviet Union wrote about "the appearance of new superpowerful means of mass destruction" and "radical changes in the conditions of political struggle" and continued: "Under these conditions, the political aims of the sides in a future world war will be achieved not only by the defeat of the armed forces, but also by complete disorganization of the enemy economy and lowering of the morale of the population" (Sokolovskiy, 1968, p. 174). According to Sokolovskiy, the Soviet Union will be forced to adopt "aims directed towards total defeat of the armed forces of the enemy with simultaneous disorganization of his interior zone, and towards suppression of the enemy's will to resist" (p. 187). Sokolovskiy stresses the point that the several goals should be achieved simultaneously: "the annihilation of the enemy's armed forces, the destruction of objectives in the rear areas, and disorganisation of the interior". The targets consist of the enemy's "military might and his economic and moral-political potential" (p. 202).

In this definition of total warfare, the emphasis is laid on the concept of the "armed nation" which must be attacked in all its sectors. That Soviet strategic intercontinental missiles threaten US cities follows from their limited numbers and the large size of their warheads; a country with a limited number of weapons cannot conduct an effective counterforce strategy. The Soviet 20-megaton warheads are characteristic of weapons aimed at cities.

If Hugo Grotius' argument that in war everything is permitted which is necessary *ad finem belli* were still valid, coercive warfare should be legitimate. It cannot be denied that terrorizing the civilian population can be militarily effective. Schwarzenberger (1968, p. 110) states: "If the necessity of war were the exclusive criterion, it would be arguable that a policy of frightfulness would be

---

[24] What these developments led to in Viet-Nam may be found in Melman *et al.* (1968).

most likely, with the minimum of effort and in the shortest time, to produce the strategic object of war."

Hitler had some success with this strategy, for example in Holland against the background of a strategically hopeless situation. Terror can be a successful tool in some circumstances, but experience has taught that it sometimes has the opposite effect and induces grim rage and blind fury. The expectation expressed in the advice of Professor Lindemann to Churchill "that having one's house demolished is the most damaging to morale", and that the bombing of the 58 German towns of over 100 000 inhabitants "would break the spirit of the people" (Birkenhead, 1961, p. 249) proved to be wrong. The bombing of Germany had little effect, nor had the bombing of Japan.[25] Extensive research into the effectiveness of bombing in World War II, including the US *Strategic Bombing Survey,* conducted directly after the war, has established that any militarily "favourable effect" on the population's morale was very slight. Nor did North Viet-Nam capitulate, despite years of bombing which surpassed in its intensity the bombing of Germany in World War II. Reactions of anger and hate can become all the more dominant if the image of the attacker undergoes a change because of the attacks on civilians.[26] It then seems particularly unattractive to surrender to such an enemy.

For Europe, with its dense population, the strategy of coercive warfare holds little attraction. It is a theory that could easily be developed in a country (for example, the United States)[27] that relies on wars not being fought on its own territory, and that is convinced of its ability to prevent the "strategic bombing" of its own cities by threatening retaliation. It is a theory that belongs to a climate created by the possession of weapons which are superior in every aspect. One can then readily understand why this theory is often vigorously rejected in Europe. Beaufre (*Colloque sur l'Etat moderne,* 1968, p. 24) equates this way of conducting a war with genocide and demands *"un code de chevalerie à l'usage des combattants. C'est notre devoir de civilisés."* The demands of civilization can all the more easily be met, now that the effectiveness of such a method can be doubted on the basis of experience. That experience amounts to this conclusion: capitulation cannot be achieved by terror if there is still military hope left. If there is no hope left, terror is unnecessary.

In view of this, the conclusion can be drawn that military necessity in the form of coercive warfare is no argument for the thesis that the rule forbidding attack on civilian populations as such should no longer be considered valid.

---

[25] For the effects of the atomic bombs dropped on Hiroshima and Nagasaki, see Röling (1971, pp. 230–47).

[26] Compare Deutsch (1968, pp. 126–30).

[27] See Thomas C. Schelling, "Nuclear Strategy in Europe" in *World Politics,* 1962, pp. 421–32, in which he emphasizes the purpose "to make the war too painful to continue", and discusses "the destruction of population centers that will not go unnoticed".

IV. *Reaffirmation of the traditional principles*

The principles in relation to practice

The practice of persistently making civilian populations targets of attack has scarcely been kept a secret. One possible exception is the atomic-bomb attack on Japan, since the first reports mentioned only the many war industries in the cities. But in later reports there was no mention of these industries and it was stated point-blank that the cities had been destroyed to force Japan to capitulate, and that this plan had succeeded. The official justification given for the bombing was derived from the idea of "coercive warfare", and there is no indication that the attack was not based on an *opinio juris ac necessitatis* in the minds of the government who ordered or permitted it.

The same applies to the post-war counter-city strategy and the weapon systems based on this concept. Many objections were made to this strategy, and from being the chief component in the theory of massive retaliation, it has instead become a component of the theory of flexible response. The objections raised were not based on the strategy's immorality or illegality; they derived from arguments about its effectiveness. If counter-city strategy had been kept secret, this could have indicated the existence of moral objections and the absence of an *opinio juris*. But it was not kept secret at all, and in fact secrecy is irreconcilable with a policy based on threat.

The view that strategic attack on civilians is legitimate is strengthened by the nature of the charges levelled at the accused in Nuremberg and Tokyo. Because the Allies practised strategic bombing, the Germans were not called to account for their "coercive warfare". Those who saw the condition of Germany at the time of the Nuremberg trials, and who were aware of what had happened to Hiroshima and Nagasaki, can readily understand that such a charge would have been impertinent.

The post-war trials almost exclusively involved the vanquished and not the victors. It has repeatedly been pointed out that only rarely were trials held for war crimes committed by members of the Allied forces. There has virtually never been a post-war trial conducted by the victors against people of their own side, in which the official methods of conducting the war were at issue. In this connection it is helpful to make a distinction between war crimes committed by individuals for selfish reasons (such as rape, robbery, and so on) against the orders and regulations of their own side – one might call this kind of criminality "individual criminality" – and the war crimes that are officially accepted or tolerated criminal practices, perpetrated in pursuance of national goals (such as not giving quarter, killing shipwrecked survivors, and so on) – one might call this kind of criminality "system criminality".[28] A soldier might be tried by his

---

[28] On this subject, see Röling (1961, pp. 336, 528–56). Telford Taylor (1974, pp. 189–207) makes a somewhat similar distinction, namely, between "combat crimes" and "non-combat crimes (such

own authorities for "individual criminality", but never for "system criminality" (in which his own authorities are involved through orders or tolerance), which is the typical object of court proceedings against the enemy (national or international).

It is of course important to bring a war criminal to justice for his own individual misconduct but it is more important to determine whether official policy followed the laws of war. In the post-war trials at Nuremberg and Tokyo, the prosecutions only dealt with "system criminality".

In these trials, virtually no proceedings dealt with violations of the laws of combat. The trials usually dealt with official violation of the laws of occupation, which was interpreted and applied with painful conservatism in the post-war judgements. Because of this, the possibility of an extremely partial development arose: on the one hand, a traditional and conservative law of occupation, and on the other, a law of combat which was adapted to the misconduct of the victor (Röling, 1961, pp. 429 ff.).

The point is whether official Allied conduct constituted a change in usage and introduced a custom which invalidated the existing rules.[29] This is a difficult problem to solve. Schwarzenberger (1968, p. 152) noted that while the Tribunal's judgement in this context "avoided any positive statement on the legality of 'independent' air warfare, it certainly did not stamp it illegal". Telford Taylor (1971, p. 140) remarked that the Nuremberg and Tokyo judgements were silent on the subject of aerial bombardment. "Whatever may have been the laws of war before the Second World War, by the time the war ended there was not much law left."

Some support for a change of opinion could also be found in the history of the attempts by the International Committee of the Red Cross (ICRC) to preserve or restore former ethical and legal values. Since 1950, the ICRC has tried to reduce the risks to the civilian population in times of war (Pictet, 1969, pp. 22–42). With this aim in mind, the Draft Rules for the Limitation of the Dangers Incurred by the Civilian Population in Time of War were drawn up in Geneva in 1956. And because international law nowhere expressly and gen-

---

as robberies, rapes and other assaults against civilians in occupied country)". "System-crimes", however, are not only committed in combat, but also during military occupation. The post-war trials mostly dealt with violation of the laws of war concerning occupation.

[29] That custom can abrogate rules of conduct does not need to be argued. One can mention as an example the *si omnes* clause in the Hague Conventions of 1907 (Article 2, Convention IV; Article 20, Convention V; Article 7, Convention VIII; and Article 8, Convention IX) which – the Nuremberg Judgement declared (Judgment of the IMT, 1946, p. 65) – had lost its validity through custom. Even the UN Charter can be altered by custom, as was Article 27. The International Court of Justice, in its Advisory Opinion concerning the legal status of Namibia, confirmed the interpretation of the Security Council concerning the voluntary abstention by a permanent member "as not constituting a bar to the adoption of resolutions". The Court considered that in this respect a general practice of the UN had developed which changed the rule according to which resolutions could only be adopted with the concurring votes of the permanent members (ICJ, 1971, p. 22).

erally prohibits attacking civilian populations as such,[30] it was thought desirable to embody this principle in the text. Article 6 of the Draft Rules, therefore began with the injunction: "Attacks directed against the civilian population, as such, whether with the object of terrorizing it or for any other reason, are prohibited." When presented to the XIXth International Conference of the Red Cross in New Delhi in 1957, however, this draft was not accepted. Resolution XIII of the Conference merely requested the ICRC to resume its activities in this field and to send the draft, together with the Conference discussion and proposed amendments, to the various governments. The governments, however, were not prepared to conclude a multilateral convention on this basis. The draft was discussed again at the XXth ICRC International Conference in Vienna in 1965. In Resolution XXVIII, the Conference solemnly declared:

that all Governments and other authorities responsible for action in armed conflicts should conform at least to the following principles:
– that the right of the parties to a conflict to adopt means of injuring the enemy is not unlimited;
– that it is prohibited to launch attacks against the civilian populations as such;
– that distinction must be made at all times between persons taking part in the hostilities and members of the civilian population to the effect that the latter be spared as much as possible;
– that the general principles of the Law of War apply to nuclear and similar weapons.

At the same time, a resolution was adopted requesting the ICRC to continue its endeavours. Consequently, on May 1967, the ICRC sent a circular to all those states which were signatories to the 1907 Hague Conventions and the 1949 Geneva Conventions, suggesting official recognition of the principles accepted in Vienna. The circular did not have the desired results; understandably, in view of the fact that the second principle accepted in Vienna is irreconcilable with deterrence based on counter-city strategy or with coercive warfare, governments were not prepared to act on these lines. For those who believed in the efficacy of nuclear deterrence, the maintenance of peace through the "balance of terror" took precedence over any concern to make any future war more humane. It is perhaps important to note here that in earlier times, too, this choice between "peace through deterrence" and "humane war" had led statesmen to resist movements to humanize warfare. In 1907, Lord Grey declared that the UK could not agree to any regulation with could "so limit the prospective liability of war as to remove some of the considerations which now restrain the public from contemplating it". Barbara W. Tuchman, referring to this statement, adds: "Translated into simpler language, this meant that Britain could not agree to anything which might, by limiting the damages of war, cause people to enter on it more lightly." (Tuchman, 1967, p. 336).

The negative experience of the ICRC is only one of a number of factors

---

[30] "This general immunity of the civilian population has not been clearly defined in positive law, but it remains, in spite of many distortions, the basis of the law of war" (Pictet, 1966, p. 53).

affecting the question of whether attacks on civilian populations as such are at present legally permissible. On the basis of the standard practice during and since World War II, Schwarzenberger (1968, p. 159) concludes that:

In view of the conduct of air warfare during the Second World War and in Viet-Nam, the inconclusiveness in this respect of relevant post-1945 treaties and the generally known preparations made by all major Powers for air and missile warfare with "conventional" and thermo-nuclear warheads, it appears impossible to state with any confidence that near-total air and missile warfare runs counter to the contemporary laws and customs of war.

Arguments for the traditional principles

Immediately before World War II, opinions on this matter were different. The United States made the following protest against the Japanese bombing of Nanking in 1937: "This Government holds the view that any general bombing of an extensive area wherein there resides a large population engaged in peaceful pursuits is unwarranted and contrary to the principles of law and humanity."[31]

The conduct of the Allies during World War II was in open violation of this principle but in Japan and Germany, such conduct was fiercely condemned. Thus a law issued in Japan on 13 August 1942 specified the death penalty for airmen who were guilty of air attacks on civilian populations. Some of the airmen who had been shot down were in fact condemned to death under this law.[32] In Germany too, airmen were apparently sentenced for bombing civilians during the war.[33]

A verdict given in Japan after the war is important here. In the case of Shimoda *et al.* – a civil action brought by Shimoda and three others, all victims of the atomic bombs, who asked for damages on the grounds of the illegality of the nuclear attacks on the civilian population – the judgement, given on 7 December 1963, dismissed the plaintiff's claims. But it did present detailed ar-

---

[31] Quoted in Giovannitti and Fried (1965, p. 37). The wording used suggests the terms of the de Martens clause.

[32] Some of the accused in the Tokyo trial were held responsible for the promulgation of that law and for the death sentence (see the Judgment of the IMT for the Far East, pp. 1024–31).

[33] See, for example, the sentence reported in Philips (1963, pp. 324, 331–35, 395–422). It should, however, be mentioned here that in his detailed and thorough investigation of sentences passed in Germany, Professor C.F. Rueter, the editor of *Justiz und NS-Verbrechen* (Univ. Press, Amsterdam), found no German judgements in which the bombing of civilian population as such was declared to be a criminal act. Many airmen were lynched on the spot, but some of those who perpetrated these lynchings were later brought to justice. The German Federal Court decided (BGH 1Str. 284–285, judgement of 18 November 1955, *Justiz und NS-Verbrechen*, No. 413c) that such reprisal lynchings were legally unacceptable. However, in the court's motives for the punishment, passages such as the following are regularly used: *"strafmildernd wurde berücksichtigt, dass der Angeklagte . . . sich über die Terrorangriffe der Alliierten gegen die Zivilbevölkerung empört haben mag . . ."* (Landgericht Koblenz 8 kr 2–61, judgement of 7 June 1962, *Justiz und NS-Verbrechen* No. 538a).

guments for why the attacks on the two Japanese cities violated international law.[34]

Another important factor was the unofficial tribunals held at Stockholm and Roskilde, where the United States was called to account and found guilty of misconduct in Viet-Nam. The practice of coercive warfare against North Viet-Nam and the brutal methods used in South Viet-Nam, notably the "fire-free zones" (later called "special strike zones" – SSZ – by the USA), were widely condemned as criminal and the news of the massacre at Song My aroused much indignation. James Reston was correct in wondering what difference it actually made whether villages were destroyed from the air or whether a group of villagers were shot down in cold blood. In human terms, however, there is a great difference, although many wanted to brand as war criminals those who gave the orders for "indiscriminate air warfare".

After World War II, spiritual leaders repeatedly condemned attacks against civilian populations. The Second Vatican Council spoke out against terror bombing. Vaticana II, Section 80 states: "Every act of war indiscriminately directed at destroying whole cities or large areas with their inhabitants is a crime against God and mankind, which deserves to be resolutely and vigorously condemned."

Instructions given to the armed forces in most countries are still based on the traditional point of view, but in the United States there is a discrepancy between the army and the navy manuals. US Army Field Manual FM 27-10 states in Section 42 that lawful military targets may be bombarded; there is no indication whether attacks on civilian populations are legitimate, as this depends on whether coercive warfare is recognized as admissible or not. Section 621 of the Law of Naval Warfare (1955) is clearer: "Bombardment for the sole purpose of terrorizing the civilian population is prohibited."

The West German regulations uphold the principles accepted in the Hague Regulations of 1907 (Articles 22 and 23e and g) and the rules of air warfare of 1923. In the German manual *Kriegsvölkerrecht. Leitsätze für die allgemeine Ausbildung* (1956, second edition 1960), coercive warfare is held to be forbidden. And the *Völkerrechtliche Grundsätze der Landkriegführung* (1961) even contains the express provision that "quasi-combatants" may not be attacked: *"Nichtkombattanten dürfen auch dann nicht unmittelbar zum Ziel eines Angriffs gemacht werden, wenn sie eine kriegswichtige Tätigkeit ausüben (z.B. Rüstungsarbeiter). Vor allem aber sind Terrorangriffe gegen die Zivilbevölkerung völkerrechtswidrig."*

Those who are concerned with preserving the rights of man have also been active in the field of maintaining human rights in times of war. The United Nations International Conference on Human Rights, held in Teheran in April and May 1968, adopted Resolution XXIII which urged the realization of the humanitarian principles. The Conference also requested the UN General As-

---

[34] The judgement is published in the *Japanese Annual of International Law,* 1964, pp. 212–52. See further Falk (1964, pp. 759–73).

sembly to sponsor studies on "steps which could be taken to secure the better application of existing humanitarian international conventions and rules in all armed conflict" and on "the need for additional humanitarian international conventions to ensure the better protection of civilians, prisoners and combatants in all armed conflicts and the prohibition and limitation of the use of certain methods and means of warfare".

On 19 December 1968 the General Assembly adopted Resolution 2442 (XXIII) (with 115 votes in favour, none against and 1 abstention), endorsing the Proclamation of Teheran. On the same day, Resolution XXVIII of the 1965 ICRC Conference at Vienna was affirmed as follows:

Affirms resolution XXVIII of the XXth International Conference of the Red Cross held at Vienna in 1965, which laid down, *inter alia,* the following principles for observance by all governmental and other authorities responsible for action in armed conflicts:
(*a*) That the right of the parties to a conflict to adopt means of injuring the enemy is not unlimited;
(*b*) That it is prohibited to launch attacks against the civilian populations as such;
(*c*) That distinction must be made at all times between persons taking part in the hostilities and members of the civilian population to the effect that the latter be spared as much as possible (General Assembly Resolution 2444 (XXIII)).

It is significant that the fourth principle of the Vienna Resolution (see page 27) – "that the general principles of the Law of War apply to nuclear and similar weapons" – was not adopted. This principle was formulated in Vienna when it appeared there would not be an acceptable majority for a condemnation of nuclear weapons, but the UN General Assembly had already spoken out more forcefully on this point. Resolution 1653 (XVI) of 24 November 1961 laid down that: "Any State using nuclear and thermo-nuclear weapons is to be considered as violating the Charter of the United Nations, as acting contrary to the laws of humanity and as committing a crime against mankind and civilization." This resolution was accepted by 55 votes in favour and 20 against, with 26 abstentions. Almost all NATO countries voted against the resolution except Norway, Denmark and Iceland, which abstained. The majority which adopted the resolution was made up of those UN members which had not formerly belonged to the circle of "civilized nations". In contrast to the countries which had once constituted the select groups of "civilized nations", these new nations appealed to the demands of civilization in rejecting the use of nuclear weapons.[35]

Finally, the opinion of the jurists is important as a subsidiary means for determining rules of law. Rather than surveying the attitudes held by the most highly qualified jurists of international law in their textbooks, the resolution

[35] Another recent resolution of the General Assembly should be mentioned here. In Resolution 2936 (XXVII) of 29 November 1972, the General Assembly solemnly declared on behalf of the Member States of the UN "the permanent prohibition of the use of nuclear weapons" (73 votes in favour, 4 against and 46 abstentions).

adopted (with only one vote against) at the meeting of the Institute of International Law at Edinburgh in September 1969[36] is cited below:

The Institute of International Law,

Reaffirming the existing rules of international law whereby the recourse to force is prohibited in international relations.

Considering that, if an armed conflict occurs in spite of these rules, the protection of civilian populations is one of the essential obligations of the parties.

Having in mind the general principles of international law, the customary rules and the conventions and agreements which clearly restrict the extent to which the parties engaged in a conflict may harm the adversary.

Having also in mind that these rules, which are enforced by international and national courts, have been formally confirmed on several occasions by a large number of international organizations and especially by the United Nations Organization.

Being of the opinion that these rules have kept their full validity notwithstanding the infringements suffered.

Having in mind the consequences which the indiscriminate conduct of hostilities and particularly the use of nuclear, chemical and bacteriological weapons, may involve for civilian populations and for mankind as a whole.

Notes that the following rules form part of the principles to be observed in armed conflicts by any *de jure* or *de facto* government, or by any other authority responsible for the conduct of hostilities:

1. The obligation to respect the distinction between military objectives and non-military objects as well as between persons participating in the hostilities and members of the civilian population remains a fundamental principle of the international law in force.

2. There can be considered as military objectives only those which, by their very nature or purpose or use, make an effective contribution to military action, or exhibit a generally recognized military significance, such that their total or partial destruction in the actual circumstances, gives a substantial, specific and immediate military advantage to those who are in a position to destroy them.

3. Neither the civilian population nor any of the objects expressly protected by conventions or agreements can be considered as military objectives, nor yet

(*a*) under whatsoever circumstances the means indispensable for the survival of the civilian population.

(*b*) those objects which by their nature or use serve primarily humanitarian or peaceful purposes such as religious or cultural needs.

4. Existing international law prohibits all armed attacks on the civilian population as such, as well as on non-military objects, notably dwellings or other buildings sheltering the civilian population, so long as these are not used for military purposes to such an extent as to justify action against them under the rule regarding military objectives as set forth in the second paragraph hereof.

5. The provisions of the preceding paragraphs do not affect the application of the existing rules of international law which prohibit the exposure of civilian populations and of non-military objects to the destructive effects of military means.

6. Existing international law prohibits, irrespective of the type of weapon used, any action whatsoever designed to terrorize the civilian population.

---

[36] Adopted on the basis of the report by Prof. Von der Heyte: *"Les problèmes que pose l'existence des armes de destruction massive et la distinction entre les objectifs militaires et non militaires en général", Annuaire de l'Institut,* Session de Nice, 1967, Vol. 52, Tome II, pp. 1–171. The text of the resolution can be found in *Annuaire de l'Institut,* Session d'Edimbourg 1969, Vol. 53, Tome II, pp. 358–60.

7. Existing international law prohibits the use of all weapons which, by their nature, affect indiscriminately both military objectives and non-military objects, or both armed forces and civilian populations. In particular, it prohibits the use of weapons the destructive effect of which is so great that it cannot be limited to specific military objectives or is otherwise uncontrollable (self-generating weapons), as well as of "blind" weapons.

8. Existing international law prohibits all attacks for whatsoever motive or by whatsoever means for the annihilation of any group, region or urban centre with no possible distinction between armed forces and civilian populations or between military objectives and non-military objects.

The validity of traditional law

The legal question remains to be answered: Is the traditional law still valid, or should it be considered as having been abolished through contrary practice in total war and through the strategic theory of the Cold War as adopted in present-day military postures? The answer to this question will indicate whether or not the atomic-bomb attacks on Japan, the bombing of North Viet-Nam, and NATO and WTO policy are to be condemned. These are matters of grave consequence.

The legal arguments that "the traditional rules distinguishing civilians and combatants no longer exist" cannot easily be dismissed. What is at issue here is the practice of the world's most powerful and influential nations. And the practice of such nations has always carried great weight in international law; these are the nations which once formed an exclusive group of "civilized countries" and which claimed on the basis of this civilization the right to rule over – and to bring "the blessings of civilization" to – others.[37]

One aspect of this civilization was the development of technology. It is the tragic fate of the "civilized nations" that the indiscriminate use of their technology proved detrimental to other demands of civilization. For this reason, a majority of 55 mainly "young countries" in the XVIth UN General Assembly accepted a resolution which impressed upon the nuclear powers that any use of nuclear weapons must be considered as a "crime against mankind and civilization".

The same Assembly gave its verdict on the admissibility of military attacks against the civilian population as such, whether as a result of a policy of deterrence or as a result of coercive warfare. With 110 votes in favour and no abstentions, Resolution 2444 (XXIII) of 1968 states "that it is prohibited to launch attacks against the civilian populations as such".

Admittedly, this resolution came from Main Committee III of the UN General Assembly and was accepted in the context of deliberations on human rights. It could be argued that it was not the Departments of the Exterior or Defence which were speaking in Main Committee III, but rather the milder

---

[37] Compare Röling (1960, p. 10); reference is made to Article 6 of the General Act of the Berlin Conference, 1886, on the Congo.

Ministries of Social Affairs. All the same, it seems that differences of opinion exist in those countries that have practised "war against civilians" and that have prepared, through their arms programmes, for such a war. The *opinio juris,* which is so important for making custom into legal precedent, is evidently divided.

There is a diversion in world opinion. On the one hand, there is the opinion that what the Euro-American World has been doing during and since World War II cannot be unjust, and has therefore become valid international law. But, on the other hand, one may wonder whether this is not a too Euro-America-centred point of view. We are living in an expanded world, in a world of "peace-loving states" (Article 4, UN Charter), in which the opinions of the former "civilized states" are no longer undisputed.

Moreover, opinion has always been divided in the Euro-American part of the world. Now that the anger against Germany and Japan has somewhat cooled and the bombing of civilians which occurred then can be judged less emotionally, distinctly different views are apparent. On one side there is the opinion of the military who, fascinated by the possibilities held out by technology, are prepared to reject the old norms. On the other side there is the growing conviction that we have taken the wrong path and have to return to former standards of civilization and humanity. A whole culture may be in error for a generation and forget its fundamental principles. It is not surprising that jurists are speaking out and refusing to recognize that an unjust practice could have developed into law. This was the position taken by the Institute of International Law in 1969, by an overwhelming majority (with only one vote, that of Jessup, against).

It is important that jurists take a clear stand. Traditional law can be reinstated. As Schwarzenberger (1968, p. 429) writes: "Governments are always free to restate or develop by way of treaty the law they have obscured beyond recognition by their own practices". They can also contribute to the restoration of former norms by changing their practices.

As a matter of fact, governments are at present in a process of treaty-making which aims at doing just that. The ICRC took the initiative to come to a reaffirmation and to a progressive development of the laws of armed combat. It drew up two Protocols to the 1949 Geneva Conventions: one concerning international armed conflicts, and a second relating to the protection of victims of non-international armed conflicts. The Protocols take as their starting point that the civilian population should be spared as much as possible. Means of combat or any methods which cannot discriminate between military objectives and civilians are forbidden, as well as attacks which injure the civilian population disproportionately (Article 46, Protocol I; Article 26, Protocol II).

During the First Session of the Diplomatic Conference on the Reaffirmation and Development of International Humanitarian Law Applicable in Armed Conflicts (Geneva, 1974), Main Committee III proposed to adopt the following text of Article 46, Protocol I: "1. The civilian population as such, as well as individual civilians, shall not be made the object of attack. In particular, methods intended to spread terror among the civilian population are prohibited."

The same text was proposed in Article 26, Protocol II for non-international armed conflicts. Both Articles 26 and 46 contain provisions prohibiting attacks on military targets which affect indiscriminately the civilian population, or which cause disproportionate civilian destruction.

It seems that jurists may conclude that the traditional norms – in which civilians as such may not be the target of military attack – have not lost their validity through contrary official practice. The traditional distinction between soldier and civilian is still the foundation of the laws of war, which means that counter-city strategy and coercive warfare are to be condemned and repudiated.

Three objections of a political and military nature can be made against this condemnation of counter-city deterrence and coercive warfare: (a) that it makes the maintenance of peace more difficult (counter-city deterrence for the sake of peace); (b) that it becomes more difficult to keep the war limited (the threat of counter-city strategy to prevent escalation); and (c) that it becomes more difficult in a war to achieve peace (coercive warfare to stimulate the willingness to come to negotiations). These arguments are put forward particularly strongly with reference to a war in Europe. Schelling (1966, p. 176) states, understandably from his point of view: "In a way, because of the greater relevance of nuclear weapons, one might put greater emphasis on brinkmanship and coercive civil damage, than on battlefield tactics, when thinking about Europe."

Are the claims of the laws of humanity and the demands of peace incompatible? It seems that the idea of "weapons for use against civilians" is wrongly credited with being an important factor in promoting the cause of peace. If it were true that survival could only be achieved by abandoning the values of civilization and humanity, then we should have to opt for survival. But this is not the choice facing us: neither the theory of deterrence nor that of coercive warfare can be credited with such importance. Whatever short-term advantages these factors may provide in the cause of peace can, and should, be dispensed with because of the harmful long-term effects they produce.

Dubious weapons

Weapons have been used in World War II, in the Korean War (even by troops fighting under the banner of the UN), in Algeria and in Indo-China which can be considered "dubious weapons" in the sense that they are morally repulsive and contrary to traditional principles, including the laws of humanity and the demands of the public conscience. Napalm and other incendiary weapons, high-velocity bullets, fragmentation weapons and delayed-action weapons have all been used in action. But all these weapons have effects that may bring them under the rules concerning unnecessary suffering, disproportionate suffering, inhumane character, and indiscriminate effects. The question is how heavily these negative features weigh, and how far the military effectiveness or military necessity may be deemed to outweigh these negative features.

The point to be stressed here is that the standards of humanity play an independent role, apart from the element of unnecessary suffering. The principle of unnecessary suffering could easily be applied to the dum-dum bullet: the ordinary bullet was designed to disable the soldier, but the special construction of the dum-dum bullet superfluously added to this "being disabled" the unnecessary suffering of having a large wound which is more difficult to treat. This superfluous suffering could be removed, while still maintaining the capacity of the weapon to disable the soldier.

With many modern weapons, this sharp distinction between the capacity to disable and to inflict superfluous injury does not exist. The small-calibre high-velocity gun, according to the military, has qualities which other guns simply do not have: light in weight, and therefore easy to carry, but greater firepower due to its increased velocity. It cannot therefore be said that the suffering is unnecessary. It is perfectly possible to produce a light-weight gun with low velocity, as for example, the US 30-calibre carbine. The problem is that while civilians claim that this weapon is relatively humane, the military claim that it is not sufficiently powerful. Inhumane suffering is inevitable if the military effect is to be produced. However, the suffering might be considered to be *disproportionate* in comparison with the military gains.

Consequently, with respect to these weapons – and the same reasoning may apply to fragmentation weapons or incendiary weapons – the question is whether the *repulsiveness* of the effect of the weapon is so great that it outweighs the military advantages. The same comparison has played a role with respect to chemical and biological weapons. It cannot be denied that the use of these weapons can be advantageous from the military point of view. But the use of these weapons is considered so repulsive and contrary to the demands of the public conscience that chemical and biological weapons have been forbidden. In regard to the present "dubious weapons", the same question must be answered: Should the demands of humanity or arguments based on military advantage prevail?

In general, it can be concluded that the traditional principles of the laws of armed combat are to be considered as still valid. The question remains to what extent these principles could lead to a prohibition of specific new weapons. Before answering this question, it must be decided whether new principles of the laws of war have already come into existence or should be recognized in the future.

V. *Progressive development of the law of war*

Proportionality

With the emergence of weapons of mass destruction, the principle of proportionality gained new significance. The thesis can be defended that already according to the traditional principles of warfare, the principle of proportionality was implied in the rules prohibiting unnecessary suffering, forbidding attacks on the civilian population as such, and prescribing to spare the civilian population as much as possible. But nowhere is this concept of proportionality expressly stated.

Now that weapons of mass destruction are available which might be used to destroy a military target but which would at the same time destroy a large city or even a large part of a country, it is more urgent to insert this concept of proportionality. Any doubt about its significance and validity in the laws of warfare should be eliminated.

It is therefore easily understood that in its Draft Additional Protocols to the Geneva Conventions of August 12, 1949 (Geneva, June 1973), the ICRC proposed specific provisions dealing with this principle of proportionality. Article 46:3*b* of Draft Protocol I, relating to the protection of victims of international armed conflicts, forbids the launching of "attacks which may be expected to entail incidental losses among the civilian population and cause the destruction of civilian objects to an extent disproportionate to the direct and substantial military advantage anticipated".

In Article 50:1*a* of Draft Protocol I, this principle was also recognized. Those who plan or decide to launch an attack should *inter alia* "ensure" (or, as an alternative proposal, "take all reasonable steps to ensure") such respect to incidental losses in civilian lives and damage to civilian objects, "that at all events those losses or damage are not disproportionate to the direct and substantial military advantage anticipated".

Article 50:1*b* prescribes that "those who launch an attack shall, if possible, cancel or suspend it if it becomes apparent that . . . incidental losses in civilian lives and damage to civilian objects would be disproportionate to the direct and substantial advantage anticipated".

At the Second Session of the Diplomatic Conference in Geneva on 3 February – 18 April 1975, Main Committee III adopted the following text:

(a) those who plan or decide upon an attack shall:
(iii) refrain from deciding to launch any attack which may be expected to cause incidental loss of civilian life, injury to civilians, damage to civilian objects, or a combination thereof, which would be excessive in relation to the concrete and direct military advantage anticipated;
(b) an attack shall be cancelled or suspended if it becomes apparent that the objective is not a military one, or that it is subject to special protection or that the attack may be expected to cause incidental loss of civilian life, injury to civilians, damage to civilian objects, or a combination thereof, which would be excessive in relation to the concrete and direct military advantage anticipated (Article 50).

This recognition of the principle of proportionality with respect to civilian damage caused by attacks, that is, to methods of warfare, also has bearing on the question of the illegality of weapons, that is, to the instruments of warfare. Future or existing weapons may be such that, by their very nature, they cause disproportionate destruction, or at least bring about the danger that such disproportionate destruction might be the consequence of their use. For example, geophysical weapons which could damage the ozone layer so that life in certain parts of the earth would become impossible are, as such, disproportionate to any military or political gain that one state or bloc of states could achieve with respect to another state or bloc of states.

In the process of evaluating new weapons, this principle of proportionality should play a role.

Survival

The modern weapons of mass destruction have introduced, moreover, a new element in the discussion of the laws of war, namely, that of survival. With the development of weapons of mass destruction – legally recognized as such in the Sea-Bed Treaty signed on 11 February 1971 as well as in the Biological Weapons Convention signed on 10 April 1972 – it became necessary to take into account the fact that total war could mean the end of civilization, possibly even of humanity itself.

Some reputable jurists, such as Julius Stone, contend that the principle of self-preservation prevails over all other rules or principles of international law.[38] According to this view, an act of war which is generally held to be unlawful is no longer so if the existence of the state itself is at stake. This is the extreme example of military necessity, where the concern is not with winning a battle but with winning a war, that is, with preserving the national existence.

As discussed above, in cases of military necessity the conduct of belligerents generally expressed the attitude that *necessitas non habet legem*. Such conduct, however – so rightly rejected by the courts – merely expressed the principle that, for the sake of military purposes, the enemy and the enemy population may be sacrificed.

The question of whether the principle of self-preservation also justifies acts which threaten the very existence of mankind did not arise in World War II. This is a new issue which has arisen with the development of biological, nuclear, thermonuclear and geophysical weapons. Only recently has it been possible to threaten with weapons whose use, if threats were to fail, would endanger mankind or a significant portion of it. This concerns not only the fate of the civilian populations in warring nations but also, through radiation or epidemic, the fate of the citizens of neutral countries, or even the fate of future generations.

---

[38] "Neither practice nor the literature explains satisfactorily how the privilege based on self-preservation in times of peace can be denied to states at war" (Stone, 1959, p. 353).

However, in international law the principle that due care must be exercised towards third parties is generally accepted, even in the law of war. It might thus be concluded *a fortiori* that acts which injure or threaten mankind are forbidden in every circumstance.

The care of mankind for the peoples which together form the human race has recently found expression in the recognition of the crime against humanity and the crime of genocide. According to national law, the killing of people has been considered a capital crime for centuries. But it was only in 1945 that the international community regarded as a crime under international law the crime against humanity. It was an expression of the opinion that the destruction of a group of people, on racial or other grounds, was a matter of concern for the whole of mankind. Mankind or the human society as a whole started action to protect its very existence by taking measures to protect its constituent parts.

The same attitude is relevant with respect to weapons which are threatening the survival of segments of humanity, if not of humanity itself. This concern for mankind as such might lead to the legal opinion even of those sharing Stone's view that in no case – even if the very existence of the state is at stake – may action be taken which might endanger the very survival of mankind or of its constituent parts.

Acceptance of this thesis does not presuppose that such rules will be observed in an extreme state of emergency; what *should* happen in that situation may be very far removed from what (probably) *will* happen. However, the firm establishment of these rules might lead to their observance in war, even in extreme circumstances. Moreover, these rules can and must be taken into account in times of peace. Their peacetime application may influence not only the development of specific strategic weapon systems but also the individual's respect for law, both among civilians and among members of armed forces. It is the latter who, most probably, will be commanded to violate the rules in times of war, and who must then refuse, according to international law, to obey the unlawful order. The most important principle of Nuremberg and Tokyo was "that individuals have international duties which transcend the national obligations of obedience imposed by the individual state". This was called "the very essence" of the Nuremberg Charter in the Nuremberg judgement (IMT, Nuremberg, 1946, p. 42).

This new consideration for the survival of mankind could have significance for determining whether specific weapons should be outlawed. Until now, this question has played only a minor role in the development of the laws of war. Expression of this new viewpoint may be found in UN General Assembly Resolution 1653 (XVI) of 24 November 1961, in which all use of nuclear weapons was condemned as "a crime against mankind and civilization", because these weapons are directed not only at the enemy but also "against mankind in general".

In its resolution on weapons of mass destruction, the Institute of International Law based its findings, *inter alia,* on the consequences which the use of nuclear, biological and chemical weapons could have "for mankind as a whole". This consideration for survival might have played a role in the 1972 Biological Weapons Convention. In its preamble, the forbidden weapons are characterized as "dangerous weapons", the use of which has to be excluded "for the sake of mankind". The first consideration which led to the 1968 Non-Proliferation Treaty concerned "the devastation that would be visited upon all mankind by a nuclear war".

It should be stressed here that the Biological Weapons Convention does not belong to the *jus in bello* but to disarmament law. The use in battle of biological weapons was already prohibited in the 1925 Geneva Protocol, and the Biological Weapons Convention extended the prohibition to the development, manufacture and stockpiling of biological weapons. In the future, prohibiting the use of specific weapons might become a normal first step in the process of prohibiting the possession of these weapons.

The environment

Related to the new value of survival is the recognition that the *environment* in which man must live deserves to be considered as a matter of concern to the whole community. The UN General Assembly, aware "that the rational management of the environment is of fundamental importance for the future of mankind" (Resolution 2849 (XXVI) of 20 December 1971), affirmed and reaffirmed "the responsibility of the international community to take action to preserve and enhance the environment".[39] It was in that connection that the General Assembly deplored "environmental pollution by ionizing radiation from the testing of nuclear weapons" (Resolution 3154 (XXVIII) of 14 December 1973).

Expressly with respect to weapons which might endanger the environment, the General Assembly adopted Resolution 3264 (XXIX) on 9 December 1974. In this resolution the General Assembly considered "it necessary to adopt, through the conclusion of an appropriate international convention, effective measures to prohibit action to influence the environment and climate for military and other hostile purposes, which are incompatible with the maintenance of international security, human well-being and health".

The ICRC did not mention the value of the environment as a factor which should be taken into account in formulating new rules of armed combat. At the First Session of the ICRC Diplomatic Conference, Australia proposed an article in Protocol I intended to protect the natural environment (ICRC, 1974, p. 46).

At the Second Session, two articles were adopted related to this issue:

[39] See, for example, General Assembly Resolution 2994 (XXVII) of 15 December 1972, and General Assembly Resolution 3129 (XXVIII) of 13 December 1973.

Article 33, Basic rules
3. It is forbidden to employ methods or means of warfare which are intended or may be expected to cause widespread, long-term, and severe damage to the natural environment.

Article 48 bis, Protection of the natural environment
1. Care shall be taken in warfare to protect the natural environment against widespread, long-term and severe damage. Such care includes a prohibition on the use of methods or means of warfare which are intended or may be expected to cause such damage to the natural environment and thereby to prejudice the health or survival of the population.
2. Attacks against the natural environment by way of reprisal are prohibited.

This article will become part of the law of armed combat. In the CCD, the USA and the USSR submitted a draft convention in August 1975 "on the prohibition of military or any other hostile use of environmental modification techniques", apparently as a step toward disarmament or arms control. A treaty forbidding the production and the possession of geophysical weapons is feasible as a freezing measure, preventing the development of this kind of weapon. However, the common draft does not forbid the manufacture of "environmental modification means", but deals rather with the prohibition of the use of such techniques. Therefore, it has the character more of new *jus in bello* than of new disarmament law, and should be mentioned here as evidence of the general opinion that the protection of the environment belongs to the recognized principles of the laws of armed conflict.

It should be noted that Article I of the 1975 draft convention prohibits "environmental modification techniques having widespread, long-lasting *or* severe effects". It goes further than the draft adopted at the Second Session of the Diplomatic Conference where the word "and" is used in place of "or". The text of article 48 bis should accordingly be altered.

It is to be foreseen that opinions will differ on the question of what kinds of weapon or what kinds of method should come under the prohibition. At the ICRC Conference, the participants were apparently thinking of the use of herbicides and techniques of defoliage, as practised in the Viet-Nam War. The draft convention of the USA and the USSR seems, according to Article 2, more inspired by the possibilities of techniques causing earthquakes, tidal waves, and weather and climate alteration, or of techniques damaging the ozone layer, and the like. In any case, both concepts take as a starting point the value of the maintenance of the ecological balance. Weapons and methods of warfare should be evaluated from this point of view. A special feature might be considered in the process of such evaluation: the fact that through the use of specific arms or through specific means of warfare, irreversible processes would be set in motion. In such cases of irreversibility there is earlier reason to qualify the damage as severe and weapons that cause such damage should be prohibited.

The environment is already threatened by certain existing modern weapons, in the first place by nuclear weapons, but also by chemical or bacteriological weapons calculated to destroy crops or to defoliate trees (herbicides). Certain of these weapons aim at the destruction of the environment, either as a means of terrorizing the civilian population, or as a means of denying the foliage that may conceal military action.

Responsibility for the environment is recognized in the modern international law of peace. It should also be recognized in times of war. The value of "the environment" and the importance of its preservation should be recognized as belonging to the factors which should be taken into account in deciding upon the laws of war concerning "dubious weapons". Less need to do this existed in former times. At present, new weapons have become available which threaten the human environment in its integer biological existence, and technological developments may bring about the possibility of causing fundamental changes in the earth's ecology. The time is ripe to brand specific acts as international crimes of "ecocide".[40] The laws of war should be adapted to this new situation.

The principle of the threshold

It is true that the use of some specific "dubious" weapons could in special situations be considered as not violating the existing principles of the laws of war. In the case of nuclear weapons, an example might be the use of some types of "mini-nukes" against missiles in outer space. The question then arises whether the general prohibition of nuclear weapons should be refused because some specific types might, in specific circumstances, be legitimate weapons.

There is a great difference between prohibiting the use of nuclear weapons in general, and prohibiting the use of a specific kind of nuclear weapon. A clear threshold divides conventional from nuclear weapons. If this threshold is trespassed, the road is open to the use of all nuclear weapons. In other words, the danger is apparent that any use of any nuclear weapon may lead to an escalation of nuclear warfare, which may end in total nuclear war.

For the sake of humanity and of survival, this threshold between conventional and nuclear weapons needs to be strengthened, even though it may lead to the outlawing of all nuclear weapons in all circumstances including those in which the use would not generally be unlawful.

The same reasoning applied to the use of tear gases. One can easily imagine circumstances in which the use of these chemical weapons would not be in violation of the traditional laws of war. But any use of gas or chemical weapons might lead to trespassing the threshold existing between conventional warfare and chemical warfare, and thus lead, through escalation, to unrestricted chemical warfare, including the use of forbidden lethal chemical weapons. Here again, the recognition of the principle of the threshold might contribute to or even be essential for the factual exclusion of forms of chemical warfare that are illegal.

[40] Compare Falk (1971, p. 348).

Conclusion and summary

Consequently, the time has come to consider the question of whether – in view of technological developments in weaponry – new principles with respect to the laws of war concerning the prohibition of specific weapons should be added to the traditional ones.

In some cases doubt may exist about whether new principles must apply, or whether rules apply which logically derive from established principles with respect to newly developed weapons.

Such principles in line with already existing principles should, however, be expressly mentioned. They should be clearly and unequivocally recognized.

1. *The principle of proportionality* would lead to the following rules: (*a*) the prohibition of weapons which cause disproportionate suffering, and (*b*) the prohibition of military acts which cause disproportionate suffering.

This principle applies in the first place to accidental civilian suffering which is disproportionate to the military gains. The proposed Article 50 of Protocol I, adopted by Main Committee III of the Second Session of the Diplomatic Conference concerning the laws of war, deals exclusively with attacks on military targets "which may be expected to cause incidental loss of civilian life, injury to civilians, damage to civilian objects or a combination thereof which would be excessive in relation to the concrete and direct military advantage anticipated".

The principle of disproportionality has not been adopted by that conference with respect to military injury and suffering. But if the rule forbidding unnecessary injury and superfluous suffering (proposed article 33:2 of Protocol I) is understood in such a restricted way that the injuries covered by that rule "be limited to those which were more severe than would be necessary to render an adversary *hors de combat*", there may be room for the principle that specific cruel injuries may be disproportionate to the military advantage of disabling a soldier. But there we might approach the field where respect for the laws of humanity would outweigh the desire for military advantage.

2. *The aspect of the survival of mankind* should be taken into account with respect to forbidden weapons or forbidden activities. This would imply: (*a*) the principle that the survival of mankind prevails over any national interest, and (*b*) the principle that in the question of whether a specific weapon should be forbidden, not only should the inhuman character of the weapon be taken into account but also the danger for the integer continuation of the human race or groups thereof.

The aspect of survival of mankind or of one or more of its constituent parts (peoples) as a factor to be taken into account has not been mentioned up till now in proposals adopted by Main Committee III. But the proposed Article 48 of Protocol I concerns the survival of the civilian population. It prohibits starvation of civilians as a method of warfare (Article 48:1) and the destruction of objects indispensable to the survival of the civilian population (Article 48:2). It prohibits the use of methods or means of warfare which may be expected

42

to cause damage to the natural environment, prejudicing the survival of the population (Article 48 bis; see also Article 33). It prohibits attack on works or installations containing dangerous forces, such as dams, dykes or nuclear plants (Article 49).

A fortiori, it seems that the survival of mankind should be recognized as a value which may lead to the prohibition of weapons or methods of warfare. In case such a value is recognized, the danger that mankind would be put in jeopardy should already be taken into account.

3. *The principle that the environment* should be taken into account with respect to forbidden weapons or forbidden activities would mean that the prohibition of specific weapons or specific action would also be based upon ecological considerations (the impact on nature, the destruction of its natural balance, the introduction of irrevocable processes).

This new aspect has been recognized by Main Committee III at the Second Session of the Diplomatic Conference, in the proposed Article 33:3, "It is forbidden to employ methods or means of warfare which are intended or may be expected to cause widespread, long-term and severe damage to the natural environment", as well as in Article 48 bis.

It was also recognized in the August 1975 US-Soviet draft concerning geophysical weapons proposed to the CCD.

4. *The principle of the threshold,* that the demands of humanity or of survival may imply the total prohibition of some kinds of weapons – notwithstanding the fact that a specific kind of use would not be contrary to the laws of war – because any use would mean a trespassing of a threshold, and would open up the road for an application of forbidden weapons by which the survival of mankind or the environment might be jeopardized.

This principle was applied at the time of the 1925 Geneva Protocol, when chemical weapons were totally prohibited. But it has never been expressly recognized. It would be advisable to do so, because some special cases could be mentioned in which the use of a specific kind of weapon would not be contrary to the principles of the law of war, but in which it would be necessary – if the states were to wish to ban that kind of weapon – to ban it totally and unconditionally.

A specific application of the threshold principle should be mentioned. Weapons may be forbidden as blind weapons, or as unnecessarily cruel weapons or as weapons which threaten the integer existence of the human environment or even of humanity itself. But weapons may exist which could be used in a way not in violation of the legal rules, but which are usually employed in such a way that they violate those rules. It may be especially characteristic for a specific weapon to be used in a forbidden way. Experience in World War II, the Korean War and the Viet-Nam War may have taught that mostly a specific kind of weapon, for example napalm, is employed in an illegal way. This may be a reason to forbid the weapon *in toto.*

In summary, all the principles of the laws of war relevant to dubious weapons may be presented as in the list below. These principles are valid today, and may all be considered as restatement, reformulation and adaptation of the traditional principles. They are pertinent to the question of whether the use of specific weapons should be outlawed.

1. Prohibited are weapons or munitions which *per se* cause unnecessary suffering to the disabled combatant.
2. The respect due to the civilian population leads to the prohibition of an attack on civilians, as such. Moreover, it leads to
    (*a*) the prohibition of weapons which cause incidental disproportionate suffering to the civilian population,
    (*b*) the prohibition of weapons which cannot discriminate ("blind weapons"),
    (*c*) the prohibition of weapons which can be expected to be used in such a way that they cause disproportionate suffering to the civilian population or that they do not discriminate between civilians and combatants.
3. The cruel and repulsive character of weapons may lead to the conclusion that the laws of humanity and the demands of the public conscience should prevail over the favourable military aspects ("military necessity"), in such a way that they are prohibited notwithstanding their military usefulness.
4. Weapons may be prohibited because they can be expected to be generally used in such a way that the laws of humanity and the demands of the public conscience should prevail over the military usefulness.
5. The treacherous character of weapons may lead to their prohibition (because they would diminish the possibility of negotiations – cease-fire, peace negotiations).
6. Weapons which violate principles of the laws of war may be regarded as legitimate weapons because they are considered indispensable for the maintenance of peace.
7. Weapons may be prohibited because they threaten the integer existence of humanity or its constituent parts, peoples or civilizations ("survival value").
8. Weapons may be prohibited because they threaten to disturb the ecological balance by causing widespread, long-lasting or severe damage to the natural environment ("environment value").
9. Weapons may be prohibited because they can be expected to be generally used in such a way that they threaten the values of survival or environment.
10. Types of weapons may be prohibited totally – although a specific kind in specific circumstances would not violate the principles of the laws of war – because any use of this type of weapons would trespass a threshold between this type and other types of weapons, and thereby create the danger, through escalation, of the general use of these weapons.

Chapter 2. Application of the principles of the law of war to new weapons

I. *Introductory remarks*

General principles *vs* specific prohibitions

It is not sufficient to formulate, in the process of the reaffirmation and progressive development of the law of war, the principles of the laws of armed conflict. These principles are of a general nature, and in many cases they amount to a recognition of specific values that may lead to the prohibition of weapons. Whether or not they result in the prohibition of specific weapons depends on such factors as the "necessities of war" or "the demands of peace", which are evaluations that are interpreted differently by the different states. It is desirable, therefore, that these evaluations of the different values and interests at stake are made at a diplomatic conference of governments. Such a conference should give its authoritative interpretation of the principles of the law of war with respect to specific weapons or specific uses of those weapons, establishing specific rules prohibiting or restricting the use of certain specific weapons or categories of weapons. For new weapons, however, even with respect to which no collective pronouncements have been made, each party to the Draft Additional Protocols to the 1949 Geneva Conventions will have to apply the principles of the law of war.

This duty is emphasized in the proposed Article 34 of Protocol I:

In the study, development, acquisition, or adoption of a new weapon, means, or method of warfare a High Contracting Party is under an obligation to determine whether its employment would, under some or all circumstances, be prohibited by this Protocol or by any other rule of international law applicable to the High Contracting Party.

The weapons to be discussed

On the initiative of the International Committee of the Red Cross, the First Session of the Diplomatic Conference on the Reaffirmation and Development of International Humanitarian Law Applicable in Armed Conflicts was convened in 1974 (see UN, 1974). The Second Session was held in 1975 (see UN, 1975), and the Third Session is scheduled for 1976. The Conference deals with *inter alia* the problem of whether certain newly developed weapons should be prohibited. It aims at formulating express prohibitions of clearly defined weapons, or of specific use of those weapons.

The Third Session of the Diplomatic Conference will restrict its deliberations to four categories of conventional weapons: incendiary weapons, small-calibre high-velocity bullets, fragmentation weapons and delayed-action weapons.

At the First Session, certain delegations criticized confining the work of the

Diplomatic Conference to certain conventional weapons. "They rejected the view that the debate on nuclear weapons and other weapons of mass destruction should be left to the disarmament discussions and urged the Diplomatic Conference to include them in its programme of work." But many other delegations accepted the limitation of the work to conventional weapons. Some pointed out that under present conditions, such weapons of mass destruction, particularly nuclear weapons, have a special function "in that they act as deterrents preventing the outbreak of a major armed conflict between certain nuclear Powers" (UN, 1974, p. 49).

It may have been a wise policy to restrict the issue of "dubious weapons" to these four categories of conventional weapons. It was considered that nothing would have been accomplished at a diplomatic conference whose aim was to consider the legality of all weapons, including weapons of mass destruction and in particular nuclear weapons. But the question of nuclear weapons still influenced the deliberations of the Diplomatic Conference. Reading the records, one has the impression that some delegations were reluctant to formulate clearly the established or newly adopted principles of the laws of armed conflict, for fear that with such a clear formulation, nuclear weapons would appear to fall within the category of forbidden weapons. In this chapter, however, nuclear weapons will be included in the short survey of all categories of weapons with respect to their legality.

Humanitarian aspects *vs* military usefulness

In applying the principles of the laws of war, the character and effects of the specific weapons must be evaluated, for example, their inhumanity, their indiscriminate effects, their impact on the environment and their inherent danger for the survival of mankind. These characteristics must in turn be weighed against the necessities of war or the presumed demands of peace. The evaluations made are strongly subjective. Opinions will differ in considering weapons possessed by the opponent alone, as opposed to considering weapons which are in the exclusive possession of one's own country. The military value attributed to a new weapon will also differ, depending on which country has the lead in its development. As in disarmament negotiations, a technological lead held by one country may promote unwillingness to agree to a prohibition. It is suggested, however, that this has proven to be an unwise policy. Since although it may take years to catch up with the technological level of an adversary, the new weapon is eventually also developed by other countries. The real question at stake is whether military necessity demands the employment of a specific weapon-type when both parties to the conflict have the weapon at their disposal. The real question is whether in that situation the military advantage of using these weapons outweighs the horrors and dangers of their use.

Reprisals

Prohibition of the *use* of a specific type of weapon (according to the law of war) should be distinguished from the prohibition of the *possession* of a specific type of weapon (according to the laws of disarmament or arms control). The layman may wonder what purpose there is in having arms that may not be used. But it should be remembered that the prohibition of the use of a weapon is no longer valid if an opponent uses that weapon. For instance, the use of chemical weapons in reprisal against the unlawful use of chemical weapons would not be illegal. To be able to use prohibited weapons in reprisal is the significance of having them in possession. History has shown that the prohibition of a weapon is often insufficient reason to abstain from its use, but that the fear of reprisals in kind may induce a belligerent to refrain from using it.

This institution of the reprisal is one of the most horrible aspects of the laws of armed combat. But in time of war it provides for almost the only sanction on violation of the law. Since in wartime no authority can enforce the law, the only sanctions are horizontal sanctions taken by the opponent: reprisal. A reprisal can be defined as action taken against an opponent, which as a general rule would be forbidden, but which is allowed in this special circumstance for the purpose of stopping the illegal conduct of the opponent. According to customary international law, reprisals are in general allowed, but there are exceptions. They are, for example, especially forbidden against the sick, wounded, shipwrecked, and against prisoners of war (1949 Geneva Convention I, Article 46; II, Article 47; III, Article 13; and IV, Article 33). The Diplomatic Conference adopted with regard to Protocol I a prohibition of reprisals with respect to attacks against civilian populations (Article 46:4), cultural objects (Article 47 bis), objects indispensable to the survival of the civilian population (Article 48), the natural environment (Article 48 bis), and against installations containing dangerous forces (Article 49).

Generally a reprisal need not be a reprisal in kind, since that is not always possible. It is, however, advisable when prohibiting specific types of weapons to state expressly that they may only be used in reprisal against the illegal use of that same type of weapon by the opponent.

If a reprisal compels the attacker to cease its illegal conduct, the reprisal has performed its function and should also cease. Herein lies the difference with a rule that would only prohibit the first use of a specific weapon, for example nuclear weapons: if a belligerent initiates the use of nuclear weapons, the opponent is then entitled to use nuclear weapons during the whole war. Therefore, the prohibition of a specific kind of weapon (leaving open the legality of its use by reprisal in kind) goes further than the prohibition of its "first use".[1]

---

[1] In several resolutions the Security Council condemned "reprisals as incompatible with the purpose and principles of the United Nations" (S/RES/188 (1964) of 9 April 1964; see also S/RES/228 (1966), S/RES/248 (1968) and S/RES/270 (1969)).

The reprisals outlawed in these resolutions refer to reprisals in peacetime, consisting of violent

The Draft Additional Protocols

The ICRC Diplomatic Conference deals not only with international armed conflicts – wars (Protocol I) – but also with armed conflicts not of an international character – civil wars (Protocol II). In both cases, but particularly in the case of civil wars, an assymetry might exist between the belligerents. It is true that the conference was called upon to deal with new weapon developments in the technologically highly developed countries. The prohibition of specific weapons or methods of combat, especially provisions which would prohibit specific weapons unless certain conditions were fulfilled, might favour the rich and technologically competent parties and rob the poor countries of their weapons. The conference must keep in mind that no convention with a discriminating effect, favouring the states which can afford to spend enormous amounts of money on weapons, would be acceptable to the majority of (poor) states. The gap that exists between the rich and the poor, the technologically developed and technologically undeveloped countries should not be further aggravated by legal provisions. On the other hand, the proposals purporting to equalize their power by legal prohibitions aimed especially at the powerful – for example, the suggestion that "the use of military air power by a party in the conflict who possesses complete air superiority" should be forbidden (see Report of the Secretary-General, para. 109) – would have little chance of being adopted. The purpose of the laws of war is not that of equalizing the power positions of the parties.

Legal prohibitions of specific weapons, for example, the prohibition of the use of weapons of mass destruction, may incidently favour the poor, because those weapons are generally only in the possession of technically highly developed countries. However, that is not the purpose of the prohibition, but rather its side-effect. The purpose is to prohibit weapons which violate recognized principles of the law of war.

II. *Dubious weapons*

The term "dubious weapons" is used to denote all the modern weapons made possible by technology which may fall within categories forbidden by the laws of war. Enormous sums of money are spent yearly on weapon research. "Military research and development – the improvement of existing weaponry and the design and development of new weapons – currently absorbs about $20 billion annually and occupies the time of about 400 000 scientists and engineers throughout the world" (SIPRI, 1974*b*, p. 141).[2] The results of this enormous

acts committed in reaction to violent acts, and done with the purpose of deterring the continuation thereof. This kind of reprisal is different from the reprisal in wartime, which, according to traditional international law, is allowed in all cases where it is not expressly forbidden.

[2] These estimates are based on material assembled in the SIPRI publication *Resources Devoted to Military Research and Devlopment* (SIPRI, 1972*a*). The USA and the USSR dominate the world's military research efforts, with outlays estimated to account for around 85 per cent of the world total (*ibid.*, p. 10).

allocation of resources are staggering; they make it almost impossible to imagine what war will be like if these new weapons are used. It should be noted that considerable effort is being spent on detection systems (needed, for example, for effective antisubmarine warfare) (SIPRI, 1974*d*) and on new delivery systems (MIRVs, MARVs, cruise missiles), up to the extent of an automated battlefield (SIPRI, 1974*b*, chaps. 9–11; SIPRI, 1975*b*, chaps. 11–13).

There are several categories of "dubious weapons": (*a*) nuclear weapons, (*b*) biological and chemical weapons, (*c*) geophysical weapons, (*d*) incendiary weapons, (*e*) small-calibre high-velocity weapons, (*f*) fragmentation weapons, and (*g*) delayed-action weapons (including booby traps). The sessions of the ICRC Diplomatic Conference do not deal with the first three categories. Here, a short analysis of the legal position of all seven categories will be given. The significance of the guiding principles of the laws of war will become more apparent if they are applied to both large and small means of warfare.

Nuclear weapons

The effects of nuclear weapons are described in the Report of the UN Secretary-General on the effects of possible use of nuclear weapons and on the security and economic implications for states of the acquisition and further development of these weapons (A/6858). The report contains the unanimous findings of a committee of experts nominated by the Secretary-General in pursuance of General Assembly Resolution 2162 A (XXI) of 5 December 1966.

These effects of nuclear weapons are well known: heat, blast and radiation (direct or through fallout). In specific cases it might be possible to avoid considerable side-effects from the destruction of the military target: for instance, if a mini-nuke explodes in anti-ballistic warfare, in outer space. But some radiation is inevitable in almost all circumstances, and in most cases the effects of fallout may be felt far away from the explosion. In general, nuclear weapons, through radiation effects, are not able to discriminate between soldiers and civilians, nor between belligerents and neutrals (and not even between the present and future generations). The fate of human beings not killed by the heat or the blast, but exposed to radiation, is horrible – a slow and painful process often leading to death. Official estimates about the effects of the two bombs dropped on the Japanese cities are that 70 000 were killed and 84 000 injured in Hiroshima, and that 27 000 were killed and 41 000 injured in Nagasaki. However, even higher estimates of the casualties are given.

Insufficient time has passed since these two nuclear disasters to determine what genetic changes, if any, were induced in the survivors. All that need be noted here is that radiation from nuclear explosions can cause genetic mutations and chromosomal anomalies which may lead to serious physical and mental disabilities in future generations.

The Secretary-General's report concludes that the effects of any all-out nuclear war observe no boundary lines. The hazards could not be confined to the powers engaged in war. The opposing forces would have to suffer both the kind of immediate destruction and the more enduring lethal effects of fallout that have already been described; but neighbouring countries, and even countries that are remote from the actual conflict, could soon become exposed to the hazards of airborne radioactive fallout precipitated at great distances from the explosion. Thus, at least within the same hemisphere, populations might suffer, through the ingestion of contaminated foods and the external irradiation due to fallout particles deposited on the ground. The extent and nature of the hazard would depend upon the numbers and types of bomb exploded. Given a sufficient number, no part of the world would escape exposure to biologically significant levels of radiation. To a greater or lesser degree, a legacy of genetic damage could be inherited by the world's population.

It is self-evident that nuclear weapons are in conflict with the principles based on the respect for civilian life and property. They have indiscriminating effects *per se,* and are inhumane, cruel and repulsive weapons. The devastation and destruction is such that in a real nuclear war, the suffering is disproportionate to the military gains,[3] because survival of the peoples involved is at stake, and the integer existence of mankind might be put in jeopardy. Nuclear explosions in the open may cause severe and perhaps irreversible damage of the environment, for example, to the ozone layer. Measured against the "necessities of war", no reasonable person would deny that in this case the values of survival and of humanity should prevail over the "demands of war".

But the main argument against the outlawing of the use of nuclear weapons is based on the "demands of peace": that nuclear weapons and the threat to use them are necessary to maintain the peace. This argument, too, is unconvincing, as thermonuclear weapons would not be used in case of a conventional war. The main function of those strategic weapons is, as we saw, no longer the deterrence of war, but the deterrence of the use of strategic nuclear weapons. This has become clear since the SALT agreements consolidated "mutual assured destruction".

The same reasoning should be applied to tactical nuclear weapons, especially in the European theatre. The use of these weapons might cause the total destruction of Europe. The only "reasonable" function of tactical nuclear weapons – as long as they exist – is to deter their use. The threat of the "first use" of tactical nuclear weapons has become incredible, since it means the beginning of a nuclear war which might end in the destruction of Europe.

This does not mean that nuclear weapons have no war-deterrent effect at all. As long as nuclear weapons exist – one might even say, as long as the knowledge of them exists – there will be a possibility that they are used, out of hatred, despair or madness, that is, irrationally. Prohibition of the use, therefore, is only a factor which contributes to the forces mobilized against the use

---

[3] For the results of nuclear war in Europe, see von Weizsäcker (1971). In case of planned total nuclear attack by one of the great powers, the other has only the choice between suicide or surrender.

of nuclear weapons. A prohibition of the use of nuclear weapons would however have an impact on the weapon posture, and would have profound influence on the present NATO philosophy of "flexible response" in which "all options", including the first use of nuclear weapons, are kept open.

In this doctrine of flexible response, it is argued that the selected use of some tactical weapons – a signal of firmness of purpose – would stop aggression, and would be indispensable for deterring the adversary. But the chances are that such a first use would open the gate for the further use of nuclear weapons, and invite an escalating process which may end in disaster. The threshold between conventional and nuclear warfare would be crossed.

The conclusion to be drawn from the analysis of the present situation is that the only rational function of nuclear weapons between nuclear-weapon states, especially the great powers, is to prevent, by deterrence, the use of nuclear weapons by the opponent. Nuclear weapons neutralize each other. But this means that the "demands of peace" are no obstacle for the prohibition of the use of nuclear weapons. On the contrary. As long as NATO and the WTO threaten each other with the first use of nuclear weapons (as they do at present), mistrust and tension will build up. A military and political recognition that nuclear weapons will only be used as a reprisal in kind against the use of nuclear weapons by the other should find expression in an agreement never to use first nuclear weapons, or, better still, in a convention prohibiting the use of nuclear weapons, except as a reprisal in kind.

The opinion that the use of nuclear weapons should be forbidden is widespread in the world, especially among the non-nuclear-weapon states. Most governments of nuclear-weapon states, or of states allied to them, are opposed to a prohibition. The conflicting views of states on the legality of nuclear weapons are probably most clearly demonstrated by the voting record of the UN General Assembly on Resolution 1653 (XVI), adopted on 24 November 1961. The resolution declared amongst other things that "any state using nuclear and thermo-nuclear weapons is to be considered as violating the Charter of the United Nations, as acting contrary to the laws of humanity and as committing a crime against mankind and civilization". It was adopted by 55 to 20, with 26 abstentions.

Resolution 2936 (XXVII), adopted on 29 November 1972, (see page 2) might indicate an increasing consensus among states on the prohibition of nuclear weapons. But it should not be overlooked that the prohibition of nuclear weapons expressed in this resolution was linked with the obligation of the member states of the United Nations not to use force. In the discussion many delegates confused the question of the prohibition of force (*jus ad bellum*) with the question of the prohibition of the use of specific weapons in armed combat (*jus in bello*). This weakens the significance of the voting, because some delegates, although voting in favour of the resolution, may have had the opinion that the use of nuclear weapons is allowed in defence against armed attack. The resolution, however, mentions the "*permanent* prohibition", which can only be interpreted as the prohibition also in cases of legitimate defensive military action.

Resolutions of the General Assembly are recommendations, and the rules they embody have no binding power. Those rules, however, are significant from the legal point of view. They are "weak norms": more than nothing, but less than law. They indicate the national auto-interpretation of the law of nations. They express the legal aspirations of the great majority of the world community; they are the basis for the *opinio juris* on which further action of states rests; and they indicate in what direction international law will develop.

A powerful minority maintains that the use of nuclear weapons is not prohibited by law. For example, Article 613 of the US Law of Naval Warfare states that "there is at present no rule of international law expressly prohibiting states from the use of nuclear weapons in warfare. In the absence of express prohibitions, the use of such weapons against enemy combatants and other military objectives is permitted." A similar opinion is expressed in paragraph 35 of the US Army's Rules of Land Warfare.[4]

From the Treaty of Tlatelolco on the non-nuclearization of Latin America, it follows that the parties considered the use of nuclear weapons legal as long as this use had not been prohibited by specific rules. In Article 3, Additional Protocol II to this treaty, nuclear-weapon states undertook not to use nuclear weapons against non-nuclearized states parties to the treaty. Such a special prohibition indicates that, without it, no prohibition exists; otherwise the Protocol would have been superfluous.

In conclusion, the time has come to outlaw the use of nuclear weapons. They violate the traditional principles of international law, and they threaten the integer existence of the human environment and of humanity itself. These survival and environmental aspects have up till now not been expressly recognized in international law. There was no need for it. But with the development of weapons of mass destruction, this aspect of nuclear weapons should play a role, together with that of their inhumanness, their indiscriminate effects and their repulsiveness. The demands of the public conscience follow the rational arguments based on self-preservation. Security for mankind in general would be enhanced by a general prohibition of the use of nuclear weapons. Such a prohibition – with its consequences for strategic philosophy and weapon posture – would facilitate the endeavours to reach arms control and disarmament in this field.

The possession of nuclear weapons is forbidden in some countries, based on peace treaties concluded after World War II, where the victor compelled the vanquished to abdicate the possession of specific kinds of weapon. The peace treaties with Hungary, Bulgaria, Romania and Finland (1947) contain a prohibition of the possession of atomic, biological and chemical weapons. The same

---

[4] See also the US Field Manuals concerning nuclear weapons, such as FM 101-31-1 *Staff Officer's Field Manual: Nuclear Weapons Employment Doctrine and Procedures;* and FM 100-30 *(Test) Tactical Nuclear Operations* (August 1971).

provision applied also to Italy, but this provision was annulled by the Allies in 1951. In the Paris Agreements of 1954, the Federal Republic of Germany accepted the obligation not to produce nuclear weapons on its territory (Protocol III, Part 1, Article 1).[5] The Österreichische Staatsvertrag also contains a prohibition on the production or possession of "ABC weapons", or on experiments with them. These prohibitions rest on "victor law", characterized by the inequality of the provisions, and not on "disarmament law", which in most cases takes equality as the guiding principle. Sometimes, however, a fundamental inequality is recognized, even in disarmament law, as in the 1968 Non-Proliferation Treaty according to which non-nuclear-weapon states, the "have-nots", become legally "have-nevers". This inequality of treatment finds its justification in the belief expressed in the preamble to the treaty: "that the proliferation of nuclear weapons would seriously enhance the danger of nuclear war". The parties to the 1967 Treaty of Tlatelolco have undertaken "to refrain from engaging in, encouraging or authorizing, directly or indirectly, or in any way participating in the testing, use, manufacture, production, possession or control of any nuclear weapon" (Article 1:2).

Other treaties prohibiting nuclear weapons in specific areas – but now as a general prohibition with respect to all states – are the 1971 Treaty on the prohibition of the emplacement of nuclear weapons and other weapons of mass destruction on the sea-bed and the ocean floor and the subsoil thereof (Sea-Bed Treaty), and the 1967 Outer Space Treaty, forbidding the placing in orbit around the earth of any objects carrying nuclear weapons or any other kinds of weapons of mass destruction, the installation of such weapons on celestial bodies or the stationing of them in outer space in any other manner. In addition, the 1961 Antarctic Treaty aimed at the non-militarization of the Antarctic region ("Antarctica shall be used for peaceful purposes only"), which implies non-nuclearization.

The reasons given for the partial prohibitions in disarmament law would also be strong reasons for the permanent prohibition of nuclear weapons, except in reprisal to the use of nuclear weapons (jus in bello). As is discussed above, such a general prohibition was opposed because the threat of the use of nuclear weapons was considered indispensable for the maintenance of peace through the "balance of terror" or, at least, the prospect for both parties of a danger of unacceptable damage and devastation. It was argued, however, that the main function of nuclear weapons had gradually become the deterrence of the use

---

[5] One may wonder why this prohibition was restricted to German territory. The purpose was made clear by the secret agreement, concluded in 1957 between the defence ministers of France (Chaban Delmas), Italy (Taviani) and FR Germany (F.J. Strauss), to cooperate in the production of nuclear weapons (see the article of former Italian ambassador to France, Pietro Quaroni (1971, pp. 70–78)). The plans came to naught with the presidency of de Gaulle. As Quaroni puts it: *"Un des premiers gestes du général de Gaulle en arrivant au pouvoir fut de laisser tomber cet accord. Cela ne fit aucun bruit à l'époque, car cet accord avait été gardé très secret, mais ceci ne diminue pas l'ampleur de ce nouvel échec."* (ibid., p. 73.)

of nuclear weapons, and not the deterrence of war. The chance that the powers might be willing to outlaw nuclear weapons is at present very small indeed. One might even say that the discussion about the progressive development of the humanitarian law of warfare at the ICRC diplomatic and experts conferences (especially with respect to indiscriminate weapons) is hampered by the fear that a specific wording might be applied to nuclear weapons. It is suggested, however, that after some time the climate will change. The SALT agreements will later be recognized as the turning point with respect to the evaluation of nuclear weapons.

Because of the political and military importance of nuclear weapons, it was often said that nuclear weapons should not be discussed in the context of the law of war, but in the CCD. The thesis here, however, is that a general prohibition of the use of nuclear weapons would enhance the chances for gradual disarmament in the nuclear field. If it is generally recognized that the function of nuclear weapons is limited to the deterrence of the use of nuclear weapons – one application of the philosophy of defensive deterrence – it may be expected that endeavours to eliminate the nuclear overkill would be more successful. The prohibition of the use of nuclear weapons may be the precondition for successful nuclear arms control and disarmament.

Chemical weapons

In the 1969 Report of the UN Secretary-General on chemical and biological weapons, "chemical agents of warfare are taken to be chemical substances, whether gaseous, liquid, or solid, which might be employed because of their direct toxic effects on man, animals and plants"; and bacteriological (biological) agents of warfare are living organisms, whatever their nature, or infective material derived from them, which are intended to cause disease or death of man, animals or plants, and which depend for their effects on their ability to multiply in the person, animal or plant attacked" (UN, 1969).

Further characteristics and effects of chemical and biological weapons will not be discussed here, but reference is made to the six-volume SIPRI study *The Problem of Chemical and Biological Warfare* (SIPRI, 1971a–c, 1973, 1974a, 1975a). The question to be dealt with here is the present legal position of these weapons.

In Article 23a of the 1907 Hague Regulations respecting the laws and customs of war on land, it is especially forbidden "to employ poison or poisoned weapons". This special prohibition expressed the general feeling that poison should be excluded as a means of warfare. The use of gas in World War I was widely criticized as violating the laws of war. Article 171 of the Treaty of Versailles treated the prohibition of gas warfare as generally understood: "the use of asphyxiating, poisonous or other gases and all analogous liquids, materials or devices being prohibited, their manufacture and importation are strictly forbidden in Germany". The provision also appears in the other peace treaties of

1919–20.[6] These provisions are evidence of the general official understanding at that time that chemical warfare was forbidden. An explicit prohibition was foreseen in the Treaty of Washington of 6 February 1922, of which Article 5 reads:

The use in war of asphyxiating, poisonous or other gases, and all analogous liquids, materials or devices, having been justly condemned by the general opinion of the civilized world and a prohibition of such use having been declared in treaties to which a majority of the civilized Powers are parties,

The Signatory Powers, to the end that this prohibition shall be universally accepted as a part of international law binding alike the conscience and practice of nations, declare their assent to such prohibition, agree to be bound thereby as between themselves and invite all other civilized nations to adhere thereto.

This treaty was concluded between the USA, the UK, France, Italy and Japan, although it never entered into force because it was not ratified by France for reasons not related to chemical weapons.

On 7 February 1923, the Convention on the Limitation of Armaments of Central American States was signed in Washington. Article 5 of the Convention states:

The Contracting Parties consider that the use in warfare of asphyxiating gases, poisons, or similar substances as well as analogous liquids, materials or devices, is contrary to humanitarian principles and to international law, and obligate themselves by the present Convention not to use said substances in time of war.

The 1925 Geneva Protocol reads:

Whereas the use in war of asphyxiating, poisonous or other gases, and of all analogous liquids, materials or devices, has been justly condemned by the general opinion of the civilised world; and

Whereas the prohibition of such use has been declared in Treaties to which the majority of Powers of the world are Parties; and

To the end that this prohibition shall be universally accepted as a part of International Law, binding alike the conscience and the practice of nations;

The undersigned Plenipotentiaries declare:

That the High Contracting Parties, so far as they are not already Parties to Treaties prohibiting such use, accept this prohibition, agree to extend this prohibition to the use of bacteriological methods of warfare and agree to be bound as between themselves according to the terms of this declaration.

The High Contracting Parties will exert every effort to induce other States to accede to the present Protocol.[7]

At the time of the League of Nations, CB warfare was considered a violation of international law. In 1938 the Assembly adopted a resolution affirming that "the use of chemical or bacteriological methods in the conduct of war is con-

[6] Article 135, Treaty of Saint Germain; Article 82, Treaty of Neuilly; Article 119, Treaty of Trianon; and Article 176, Treaty of Sèvres.

[7] For the list of signatures and ratifications, see SIPRI (1975, pp. 532 ff.). The total number of actual parties to the Geneva Protocol, as of 31 December 1974, was 93. The USA became a party on 10 April 1975.

trary to international law". During World War II the parties abstained from CB warfare, probably out of fear for reprisals in kind. The indictment in the trial of major war criminals before the International Military Tribunal for the Far East contained an accusation of chemical warfare. In Appendix D to the indictment concerning conventional war crimes, Particulars of Breaches are given in Section Nine:

Employing poison, contrary to the International Declaration respecting Asphyxiating Gases signed by (inter alia) Japan and China at the Hague on the 29th July 1899, and to Article 23(a) of the said Annex to the said Hague Convention, and to Article 171 of the Treaty of Versailles:

In the wars of Japan against the Republic of China, poison gas was used. This allegation is confined to that country. (Judgment of the IMT for the Far East, 1948, Annex I, p. 116)

In this indictment the Geneva Protocol was not mentioned as a treaty violated by Japan, because Japan was not a party to it. In the Judgment of this International Military Tribunal, no findings were made concerning these accusations.

After the war, the question of the prohibition of CBW has been considered in various bodies of the UN in connection with disarmament efforts. In Resolution 2162 (XXI), adopted on 5 December 1966, the General Assembly called for the "strict observance by all States of the principles and objectives of the Protocol for the Prohibition of the Use in War of Asphyxiating, Poisonous or Other Gases, and of Bacteriological Methods of Warfare signed at Geneva on 17 June 1925, and condemns all actions contrary to those objectives", and invited all states to accede to the Protocol. The General Assembly reiterated its call for "strict observance by all States of the principles and objectives of the protocol" in Resolutions 2454 (XXIII) and 2827 (XXVI). In Resolutions 2853 (XXVI) and 3032 (XXVII) it called upon "all parties to any armed conflict" to observe the rules laid down in the Protocol.

Whatever the effect of General Assembly resolutions in international law, the affirmative votes of a majority of parties to the Geneva Protocol may be regarded as reflecting the interpretation placed on the treaty by states which are parties to the instrument. As far as the type of prohibited chemical and bacteriological weapons are concerned, in Resolution 2603 (XXIV) the General Assembly declared as "contrary to the generally recognized rules of international law" as embodied in the Geneva Protocol, the use in international armed conflicts of:

(*a*) Any chemical agents of warfare – chemical substances, whether gaseous, liquid or solid – which might be employed because of their direct toxic effects on man, animals or plants;

(*b*) Any biological agents of warfare – living organisms, whatever their nature, or infective material derived from them – which are intended to cause disease or death in man, animals or plants, and which depend for their effects on their ability to multiply in the person, animal or plant attacked.

The significance of these resolutions lies in the fact that they indicate how the Geneva Protocol was understood by a large majority of the members of the UN. This interpretation by the UN is important, especially in regard to three points in dispute.

First of all, the resolutions take the line that *all* states are bound by the provisions of the Protocol, and not only the parties to the Protocol. Second, they consider that *all* chemical weapons are forbidden, not only the lethal chemical weapons. Third, they regard as forbidden those chemical weapons which are employed because of their direct toxic effects on man, *animals or plants*.

Lawyers differ in opinion about the significance of General Assembly resolutions in which an interpretation is given of the provisions of a treaty to which not all UN members are parties. But the importance of the opinion that the provisions of the Geneva Protocol are to be regarded as rules of customary law, binding all states, cannot easily be denied. And if the provisions of the Protocol are seen as a formulation of customary law, there is less reason for denying the competence of the members of the UN to express themselves about the existing *opinio juris* which is an essential part of custom as a source of law.

The question of whether or not the words "asphyxiating, poisonous or other", which appear in the definition of the prohibited weapons in the Protocol, cover incapacitating agents in general and irritant agents in particular has a long history. The issue was raised on 2 December 1930 by the British delegation to the Preparatory Commission for the League of Nations Disarmament Conference which submitted a memorandum concerning, amongst other things, the applicability of the Geneva Protocol to the question of the use of tear gases in war. The memorandum recalled that the Protocol contains a discrepancy between the French word *similaires* and the English translation as "other" gases. It declared that, basing itself on this English text, "the British government have taken the view that the use in war of 'other' gases, including lachrymatory gases, was prohibited" (League of Nations, 1931, p. 311). Similarly, the French delegation made the following statement:

The French government therefore considers that the use of lachrymatory gases is covered by the prohibition arising out of the Geneva Protocol. . .

The fact that, for the maintenance of internal order, the police, when dealing with offenders against the law, sometimes use various appliances discharging irritant gases cannot, in the French delegation's opinion, be adduced in a discussion on this point, since the Protocol or Convention in question relates only to the use of poisonous or similar gases *in war*. (*ibid*.)

This interpretation was accepted by a number of other delegations, and was also supported by a number of other states that subsequently ratified the Geneva Protocol.

No state has at any time, either before or after 1930, ratified or acceded to the Geneva Protocol with a reservation limiting the types of chemical weapons to which it applies. The fact that the states acceding to the Protocol after 1930 did not enter a reservation excluding tear gas from the scope of the Protocol is particularly important because they had been clearly alerted to the interpretation of the treaty in that respect. Having this in mind, it might be supposed that the question of the prohibition of the use of tear gases in war under the Geneva Protocol had been definitely settled in the 1930s in favour of the broader interpretation.

It should be emphasized that already in 1930 reference was made to the fact that this means of combat against enemies would be forbidden, although the police use against compatriots was allowed. The point is that in wartime, tear gases may be used with the purpose of killing people once they have come into the open. If the police use tear gas, this is not the case. A second and more important difference is that if these gases are used in war, the danger exists that through escalation in gas warfare, lethal gases will be used. Such danger of escalation does not exist in police use for riot control. On the battlefield the use of any gas indicates that a threshold is crossed separating conventional weapons from chemical weapons, which leaves open the road for wider use of chemical weapons. Following the revival of interest in the late 1950s and early 1960s in the United States in so-called incapacitating weapons and, subsequently, the use of sensory irritant-agent weapons on a large scale in Viet-Nam, this broad interpretation has been called into question again and has become the subject of considerable controversy. Although the restrictive interpretation by the USA was endorsed by certain parties to the Geneva Protocol (Australia, Belgium and the UK), it should be recalled that, at the time, the USA was not a party to the Geneva Protocol and consequently the statements of the US government had, of course, no legal effect on the interpretation of the treaty. Nor does the practice followed by the USA relative to the military use of irritant-agent weapons have any implication for its prohibitory scope. The convictions of Australia and the UK that these or some of these weapons are now legitimate means of warfare conflict with their view in 1930 when they had explicitly endorsed the broad interpretation.

The USA has now acceded to the Geneva Protocol; the instrument of ratification was deposited with the French government on 10 April 1975. In connection with this accession, Executive Order 11850 renounced as "a matter of national policy":

first use of herbicides in war except use, under regulations applicable to their domestic use, for control of vegetation within U.S. bases and installations or around their immediate defensive perimeters, and first use of riot control agents in war except in defensive military modes to save lives such as:

(a) Use of riot control agents in riot control situations in areas under direct and distinct U.S. military control, to include controlling rioting prisoners of war.

(b) Use of riot control agents in situations in which civilians are used to mask or screen attacks and civilian casualties can be reduced or avoided.

(c) Use of riot control agents in rescue missions in remotely isolated areas, of downed aircrews and passengers, and escaping prisoners.

(d) Use of riot control agents in rear echelon areas outside the zone of immediate combat to protect convoys from civilian disurbances, terrorists and paramilitary organizations.

The use of herbicides to clear areas around US bases or their defensive perimeters would seem not to be a use in "war" in the sense of combat against the enemy. Two of the proposed uses concern the maintenance of order in areas under US control and are thus analogous to domestic uses. The use of riot-control agents in riot-control circumstances and for protection of convoys in the situations specified cannot be considered as a use in war. However, use in a situation where civilian casualties can be reduced or avoided, or use in rescue missions are both clearly uses in war. Both will take place during combat. In rescue missions riot-control agents would normally be used in conjunction with other weapons to suppress enemy fire.

As this interpretation is not part of the formal instrument of ratification, but "a matter of national policy", it cannot be formally challenged by other parties to the Protocol. But this interpretation has at least two shortcomings: first, it could be subject to change by the President or his successor, and second, it does not afford sufficient protection to the United States because a state or states not agreeing to the US interpretation might consider that the USA has violated the Protocol. This could lead to the retaliatory use of far more devastating chemicals by a state claiming that it is acting in full conformity with the law. In this respect it should be mentioned that the use of chemical weapons is allowed as reprisal in kind against the use of these weapons. This right of reprisal – generally recognized in international law in all cases where it is not expressly forbidden – should be restricted expressly to reprisals in kind. If it were allowed to use chemical weapons as reprisal against any violation of the laws of war by the adversary, any party in a conflict could initiate chemical warfare as soon as it seemed militarily advantageous. In every war the laws of war are violated, and history shows that forbidden weapons or forbidden methods of warfare have often been introduced or used under the guise of reprisals.

Biological weapons

In the indictments of the Nuremberg and Tokyo trials, no mention was made of biological warfare. After the 1948 Tokyo trial of major war criminals was terminated, the USSR initiated proceedings against Japanese generals who were prisoners of war. In the trial of Khabarovsk (Materials, 1950) on 25–30 December 1949, the defendants were accused of bacteriological warfare, and sentenced for this violation of the law of war. The verdict rested principally on the statements of the accused, in which some of them declared that the command to prepare bacteriological weapons was given by the Emperor (see for example, *ibid.,* pp. 417, 519).

At the main trial in Tokyo, however, no evidence was given on bacteriological warfare. For those who are familiar with the character of Japanese generals, it is amazing to be told that they would accuse the Emperor of war crimes. The main trouble in the Tokyo trial was that the accused generally disregarded in their statements their own interests for the sake of the honour of Japan and its Emperor. In any case, a condemnation of the manufacture of biological weapons is remarkable, because the possession of these prohibited weapons was not forbidden. States could consider it necessary to possess those weapons for the purpose of deterring, by way of the threat of reprisal, the use of such kind of weapons by the opponent. The records of Khabarovsk do not indicate that in the war against China the Japanese used bacteriological weapons. The trial may be seen, however, as evidence that the Soviet Union considered bacteriological warfare as a violation of the laws of war.

The biological weapons have characteristics of their own. According to the 1969 Report of the UN Secretary-General, the idea that bacteriological (biological) agents are potentially unconfirmed in their effects, both in space and in time, and that their large-scale use could conceivably have deleterious and irreversible effects on the balance of nature, adds to the sense of insecurity and tension which the existence of this class of weapons engenders. Were these weapons ever to be used on a large scale in war, no one could predict how enduring the effects would be and how they would affect the structure of society and the environment in which we live. This overriding danger would apply as much to the country which initiated the use of these weapons, as to the one which was attacked, regardless of which protective measures it might have taken. A particular danger also derives from the fact that any country could develop or acquire, in one way or another, a capability in this type of warfare. The danger of the proliferation of this class of weapons applies as much to the developed as it does to the underdeveloped countries.

These considerations may have contributed to the willingness of the powers to prohibit – as "a first possible step towards the achievement of agreement on effective measures also for the prohibition of the development, production and stockpiling of chemical weapons" – "to develop, produce, stockpile or otherwise acquire or retain" biological weapons, including their means of delivery. This prohibition is formulated in Article 1 of the 1972 Biological Weapons Convention, the only real disarmament treaty concluded so far, the others being only treaties which freeze the *status quo* or which put a ceiling on further armaments.

Disarmament treaties have an impact on the laws of war in that if possession of weapons is forbidden, *a fortiori* the use of these weapons is prohibited. In the case of biological weapons, the prohibition of the use in the *jus in bello* has preceded the prohibition of the possession in disarmament law.

The Biological Weapons Convention will also be in force in times of war.

The answer to the question of whether or not an arms control or disarmament treaty will only be applicable in time of peace depends on the wording of the treaty and the intention of the parties. It follows, for instance, from the text of the Test Ban Treaty that the treaty lapses in times of nuclear war, because it forbids any "nuclear explosion" except underground (Article I) and it was never the intention of the parties to prohibit, in this treaty, the use of nuclear weapons in time of war. But in the Biological Weapons Convention the parties undertake "never in any circumstances" to develop, produce, stockpile or otherwise acquire or to retain biological weapons, determined, as is stated in the preamble, "for the sake of mankind, to exclude completely the possibility of bacteriological (biological) agents and toxins being used as weapons". This absolute prohibition includes the use of biological weapons as a reprisal in kind, which is a rare exception to the general rule concerning reprisals. Probably the thought has been that reprisals would be taken by means of nuclear weapons. If this has been the intention and understanding of the parties, a special provision on this point would be necessary if the use of nuclear weapons were prohibited.[8]

The prohibition of the use of biological weapons has still another exceptional feature: there is no arrangement made for inspections to verify the mutual fulfilment of the treaty provisions. If there arises any suspicion that any other state party to the Biological Weapons Convention is "acting in breach of obligations deriving from the provisions of the convention", a complaint may be lodged with the UN Security Council, and each party has undertaken to cooperate in carrying out any investigation which the Security Council may initiate (Article VI). However, where allegations concern any of the permanent members or their clients, the investigation may be vetoed. Thus, verification by investigation is not ensured by the treaty provisions. Apparently, the parties preferred to conclude a treaty with no provision for inspection to not concluding a treaty at all. The USA took a unilateral decision in 1969 to destroy its biological and toxin weapons, and later stated that the destruction of all stocks of biological and toxin agents and of all associated munitions had been completed (American Chemical Society, 1973, p. 438).

The convention entered into force on 26 March 1975, the same day that the instruments of ratification of the Biological Weapons Convention were deposited by the USA, the UK and the USSR (SIPRI, 1975*b*, pp. 591–92). The convention represents, according to its preamble, "a first possible step towards the achievement of agreement on effective measures also for the prohibition of the development, production and stockpiling of chemical weapons". One specific type of chemical weapon, the toxins, is already included in the treaty. They are included because their method of production is similar to that of biological weapons.

Geophysical weapons

Main Committee III of the Second Session of the ICRC Diplomatic Conference adopted Article 48 bis on protection of the natural environment.

---

[8] Kalshoven (1972, p. 348) concluded from the many reservations to the Geneva Protocol that "the unqualified prohibition laid down in the Protocol" had been virtually reduced "to a prohibition on condition of reciprocity", and that "under the terms of the Protocol and reservation thereto, and within the limits imposed by ... general rules, a belligerent is fully entitled to use chemical or biological weapons if the enemy had made use of nuclear weapons". Since the Biological Weapons Convention, this conclusion is no longer correct with respect to biological weapons.

1. Care shall be taken in warfare to protect the natural environment against widespread, long-term and severe damage. Such care includes a prohibition of the use of methods or means of warfare which are intended or may be expected to cause such damage to the natural environment and thereby to prejudice the health or survival of the population.

2. Attacks against the natural environment by way of reprisal are prohibited.

This was the first time that a prohibition of means of warfare motivated by care for the natural environment was adopted. Awareness that such a prohibition was already overdue followed upon the bitter experience of the Viet-Nam War in which, for reasons of military expediency, large regions were defoliated and crops destroyed, with devastating consequences for the ecological balance (SIPRI, 1976).

Article 48 bis prohibits methods or means of warfare, causing widespread, long-term and severe damage to the natural environment. It has proven impossible to avoid such rather vague criteria as "widespread", "long-term" and "severe". In the US-Soviet Draft Convention on the Prohibition of Military or any other Hostile Use of Environmental Modification Techniques submitted in 1975 to the CCD, "techniques having widespread, long-lasting *or* severe effects are mentioned.[9] This latter formulation deserves preference. "Long-lasting" indicates better what is meant by "long-term". And if the effects are "severe damage", the other criteria should have no restrictive influence on the prohibition.

Neither Article 48 bis nor the US-Soviet draft convention mention the element of irreversibility of the caused processes. In case of irreversible damage, there would be even an earlier reason to consider the damage "severe".

It should be noted that the protection of the natural environment will be discussed at conferences concerning the laws of war and concerning disarmament law. It would seem therefore that specific weapons exist or might be invented which have the described disastrous effects on the natural environment. The

---

[9] The texts of the first three articles of this Draft Convention read:

ARTICLE I
1. Each state Party to this Convention undertakes not to engage in military or any other hostile use of environmental modification techniques having *widespread, long-lasting* or *severe effects* as the means of destruction, damage or injury to another State Party.
2. Each State Party to this Convention undertakes not to assist, encourage or induce any State, group of States or international organization to engage in activities contrary to the provision of paragraph 1 of this article.

ARTICLE II
As used in Article I, the term "environmental modification techniques" refers to any technique for changing – through the deliberate manipulation of natural processes – the dynamics, composition or structure of the earth, including its biota, lithosphere, hydrosphere, and atmosphere, or of outer space, so as to cause such effects as earthquakes and tsunamis, an upset in the ecological balance of a region, or changes in weather patterns (clouds, precipitation, cyclones of various types and tornadic storms), in the state of the ozone layer or ionosphere, in climate patterns, or in ocean currents.

ARTICLE III
The provisions of this Convention shall not hinder the use of environmental modification techniques for peaceful purposes by States Party, or international economic and scientific co-operation in the utilization, preservation and improvement of the environment for peaceful purposes.

US-Soviet Draft does not mention specific weapons, but "environmental modification techniques", which term refers to "any technique for changing – through the deliberate manipulation of natural processes – the dynamics, composition or structure of the earth, including its biota, lithosphere, hydrosphere, and atmosphere" (Article II). The purpose is clear: The provision aims at prohibiting the use of the forces of nature for hostile purposes: using earthquakes, tidal waves, the rays of the sun (by removing the protection of the ozone layer), ocean currents and climate as means of injuring the enemy. The forces which set in motion these "natural powers", that is, the "environmental modification techniques" are the objects of the prohibition. In that respect the prohibitions aimed at have some equivalence with Article 49 of Draft Additional Protocol I: "It is forbidden to attack or destroy works or installations containing dangerous forces, namely, dams, dykes and nuclear generating stations. These objects shall not be made the object of reprisals."

In the US-Soviet Draft it is the unleashing of natural forces, while in Article 49 it is the unleashing of unnatural, man-made forces which will be forbidden. It might seem, therefore, that in both cases specific conduct is forbidden, which is rather the field of the laws of war.

But to deal with "environmental modification techniques" in a disarmament committee might have specific significance. The issue concerns technical developments about which Brezhnev has made ominous statements, suggesting that weapons far worse than nuclear weapons might be developed. Still, the US-Soviet Draft mentions developments in techniques and in know-how. Arms control in this field might mean regulation and control of arms research. Therefore, the above observation that the US-Soviet Draft concerns in the first place the laws of war does not mean that this issue should not be dealt with by the CCD. Rather, it might lead to the suggestion that Article 49 would be expanded to cover also "works of nature containing dangerous forces".

Incendiary weapons[10]

In the Report of the UN Secretary-General on Napalm and other Incendiary Weapons and all Aspects of their Possible Use (UN, 1973b) incendiary weapons are defined as weapons which depend for their effects on the action of incendiary agents. These are defined in turn as substances which affect their targets primarily through the action of flame and/or heat derived from exothermic chemical reactions; these reactions, for all practical purposes, are combustion reactions. The production of poisonous substances and certain other side-effects may also cause significant harm to the target.

In addition to the damage inflicted on an enemy, his possessions or his environment primarily through the action of heat and flame, incendiary weapons

---

[10] For further data on incendiary weapons, see ICRC (1973a, pp. 55–64); SIPRI (1972c); SIPRI (1974c); SIPRI (1975b) and Swedish Working Group (1973).

may also have other damaging effects: some are poisons, whilst others produce toxic or asphyxiating effects when they burn. The additional long-term ecological consequences, which could be severe, are largely unpredictable.

Incendiary agents can be grouped into four broad categories: metal incendiaries, pyrotechnic incendiaries, pyrophoric incendiaries and oil-based incendiaries. Many metals react readily with oxygen or air, generating much heat in the process. Because they are made of dense material, they may make efficient intensive-type incendiaries. Magnesium is the best-known metal incendiary.

Pyrotechnic incendiaries, such as thermite, are inflammable mixtures comprising a fuel and an oxidizing agent. They differ therefore from the other categories of incendiaries in that they incorporate their own source of oxygen and do not rely on the surrounding air for combustion. Pyrophoric incendiaries are materials which ignite spontaneously when exposed to air. This property obviates the need for special igniters. Pyrophoric incendiaries are used on their own or in conjunction with other incendiaries (such as white phosphorus and certain organometallic compounds).

The fourth category includes napalm and other oil-based incendiaries. Hydrocarbons derived from petroleum oil are inflammable liquids which possess a high heat of combustion and produce a large flame. Hydrocarbons burning in quantity frequently generate large amounts of carbon monoxide, which is a highly poisonous gas that may significantly add to the offensive properties of oil-based incendiaries. Petroleum hydrocarbons have a considerably greater heat of combustion than that of magnesium or white phosphorus. However, those which are sufficiently volatile to ignite easily, such as petrol, burn so rapidly that when dispensed by a propellant charge, they are consumed in one large and relatively harmless flash. For this reason, petrol is mixed with certain additives when used as an incendiary agent. These greatly increase its destructiveness. They modify its flow properties into a form more suited to weapons, and make it sufficiently adhesive and cohesive to stick to surfaces in burning globules. They may also prolong its burning time and increase its burning temperature. It is to this category that napalm belongs. The term napalm is now used to describe any gelled hydrocarbon incendiary.

There exists today a broad range of incendiary weapons designed for use both on the battlefield and against population centres and other vital targets. Many of these weapons are extremely simple to manufacture and the necessary raw materials are readily available the world over. This is particularly true of napalm weapons, which are already a part of the arsenals of a number of countries.

Massive use of incendiary weapons creates fires that may merge and grow into widespread conflagrations and fire storms. Such fire storms are largely uncontrollable. It follows from this, and from past wartime experience, that incendiaries are among the most powerful means of destruction in existence, characterizing the savage and cruel consequences of total war.

The massive spread of fire is largely indiscriminate in its effects. When there

64

is a difference between the susceptibility to fire of military and civilian targets, it is commonly to the detriment of the latter. The same applies to certain tactical applications of incendiaries, for the ability of these weapons to strike over an appreciable area, and the often close proximity of military and civilian targets, may also have consequences that are essentially indiscriminate.

Burn injuries, whether sustained directly from the action of incendiaries or as a result of fires initiated by them, are intensely painful and, compared with the injuries caused by most other categories of weapons, require exceptional resources for their medical treatment.

Legal opinions about incendiary weapons differ, partly because a distinction can be made between anti-personnel and anti-material incendiary weapons. The implication of this distinction is that incendiaries used only against personnel might be prohibited, and others not.

Although in World War I incendiary weapons of various types were used on all sides, the main attention after the war leading to the Geneva Protocol was directed to the use of asphyxiating and other gases. In this respect it is interesting to note that the Commission of Jurists which drew up the Hague Air Warfare Rules of 1923 stipulated in Article 18 of this code, which never entered into force, that "the use of tracer, incendiary or explosive projectiles by or against aircraft is not prohibited, and that this provision applied equally to all States whether or not they were parties to the Declaration of St Petersburg of 1868".

The Geneva Disarmament Conference of 1932–33 gave considerable attention to the question of incendiary weapons, and determined that they should be included with chemical and bacteriological weapons in qualitative disarmament. The Draft Disarmament Convention, presented at the end of the conference without opposition, would have explicitly forbidden the use of projectiles specifically intended to cause fire, and appliances designed to attack persons by fire.

The uses of incendiary weapons during World War II demonstrated their awesome possibilities to all parties. Incendiaries developed from the unreliable devices of World War I into major weapons for both tactical and strategic warfare. During the Korean War, napalm and other incendiary weapons were used by the troops fighting under the UN flag. The extensive use of napalm by US troops in the Viet-Nam War, and the pictures of the effects on the native population, contributed to the growing feeling of disgust with respect to this weapon. It clearly contradicted the "demands of the public conscience", and was widely felt to be against "the laws of humanity". From the published pictures, awareness grew that this type of weapon was having indiscriminating effects and was usually employed in an illegal manner.

In its Draft Rules for the Limitation of the Dangers Incurred by the Civilian Population in Time of War (Geneva, 1956), the ICRC proposed in Article 14 a prohibition against the use of "weapons whose harmful effects – resulting in particular from the dissemination of incendiary, chemical, bacteriological, radioactive or other agents – could spread to an unforeseen degree or escape, either in space or in time, from the control of those who employ them, thus endangering the civilian population."

The commentary accompanying Article 14 pointed out that incendiary weapons "are sometimes limited in their effect e.g. the flame-thrower or napalm when used against a tank, but sometimes have incontrollable consequences as in the case of certain bombs scattering inflammable material over a considerable distance."

The Draft Rules were the object of discussion in the XIXth International Conference of the Red Cross, held in New Delhi in 1957, but with regard to Article 14 *the discussion was entirely concentrated on the use of nuclear weapons.* Neither incendiary weapons in general, nor napalm in particular, were so much as mentioned in the debate. It was apparent that the time was not yet ripe for a prohibition of nuclear weapons, and the confusion of incendiary with radioactive agents prevented any results with respect to incendiary weapons.

After the successive adoptions of Resolution XVII at the XXth ICRC Conference (Vienna, 1965), of Resolution XXIII of the UN International Conference of Human Rights (Teheran, 1968), and the endorsement of this resolution in General Assembly Resolution 2444 (XXIII) in 1968, the road was open for new initiatives.

On the basis of the results of an expert conference on napalm and other incendiary weapons, the ICRC concluded that for the time being, and without prejudice to any total prohibition formulated subsequently, the only practicable course open to the ICRC was to concentrate on restrictions on the use of incendiary weapons.

In November 1969, the Secretary-General of the United Nations endorsed this conclusion:

Reminders to parties to conflicts that in any event the employment of incendiary weapons, such as napalm, should be accompanied by special precautions to prevent them from unduly affecting members of the civilian population or disabled members of the armed forces, or causing unnecessary suffering to combatants would therefore appear to be desirable. Moreover, in view of the reference to napalm in the Teheran Conference resolution, the legality or otherwise of the use of napalm would seem to be a question which would call for study and might be eventually resolved in an international document which would clarify the situation (UN document A/7720, 20 November 1969, para. 200).

In his second report of September 1970 on the same subject, the Secretary-General elaborated the idea of further study of the effects of napalm on human beings and the environment, and suggested that a report be prepared on the matter, with the aid of qualified experts. This idea was taken up in the XXVIth Session of the General Assembly in December 1971, and the scope of the proposed report was extended to cover "other incendiary weapons" in addition to napalm (Resolution 2852 (XXVI), 20 December 1971, para. 5).

After the Secretary-General's report was submitted, the General Assembly adopted Resolution 2932 A (XXVII) of 29 November 1972 deploring "the use of napalm and other incendiary weapons in all armed conflicts". Further, the resolution considered that "the massive spread of fire through incendiary weapons is largely indiscriminate in its effect on military and civilian targets"; that burn injuries are extremely painful and require facilities for treatment that are beyond the reach of most countries; and that such weapons pose a threat to "the long upheld principle of the immunity of the non-combatant".

In the Draft Additional Protocols to the Geneva Conventions of August 12, 1949 (ICRC, 1973b), which form the basis of the discussions of the Diplomatic Conference, the ICRC formulated principles of the laws of armed combat, without going into the express prohibition of specific weapons. At the First Session of the Diplomatic Conference (Geneva, 1974) the question of the prohibition of the use of incendiary weapons was discussed in an *Ad hoc* Committee of the whole on weapons.[11] The need was felt for further expert opinion. At the Conference of Governments Experts on the Use of Certain Conventional Weapons held in Lucerne in 1974, the question of incendiary weapons was again discussed. Although difference of opinion among the experts still existed, the prevailing thought seems to have been not a prohibition of specific methods of use of incendiary weapons, but a general prohibition of incendiary weapons with exceptions.

This was also the structure of the proposal submitted during the First Session of the Diplomatic Conference by a group of states (working paper CDDH-DT.2, submitted by Austria, Egypt, Mexico, Norway, Sudan, Sweden, Switzerland and Yugoslavia) with respect to incendiary weapons. It was largely modelled upon Article 48 of Part 4 of the British draft disarmament convention of 16 March 1933. A revised version of this proposal – sponsored by Algeria, Austria, Egypt, Iran, the Ivory Coast, Lebanon, Lesotho, Mali, Mauritania, Mexico, New Zealand, Norway, the Sudan, Sweden, Switzerland, Tunisia, the United Republic of Tanzania, Venezuela, Yugoslavia and Zaire – is proposed to the Diplomatic Conference. It reads:

1. Incendiary weapons shall be prohibited for use.
2. This prohibition shall apply to:
   the use of any munition which is primarily designed to set fire to objects or to cause burn injury to persons through the action of flame and/or heat produced by a chemical reaction of a substance delivered on the target. Such munitions include flame-throwers, incendiary shells, rockets, grenades, mines and bombs.
3. This prohibition shall not apply to:
   (a) munitions which may have secondary or incidental incendiary effects, such as illuminants, tracers, smoke or signalling systems.

---

[11] The mandate of the *Ad hoc* Committee was "to examine the question of prohibition or restriction of use of specific categories of conventional weapons which may cause unnecessary suffering or have indiscriminate effects". "Unnecessary suffering" and "indiscriminating effects" were the main principles embodied in the Draft Additional Protocols (Articles 33, 34 and 46 of Protocol I; and Articles 20 and 26 of Protocol II). This mandate did not exclude the application of other principles, included already in the Draft Protocols, or added to them by the Diplomatic Conference.

(b) munitions which combine incendiary effects with penetration or fragmentation effects and which are specifically designed for use against aircraft, armoured vehicles and similar targets.[12]

During the debate in the *Ad hoc* Committe on Conventional Weapons, it appeared that opinions were divided about the qualities and effects of the discussed incendiary weapons. The need was felt for a second conference of government experts, which "should focus on such weapons as would have been – or might become – the subject of proposed bans or restrictions, and study the possibility, contents and form of such proposed bans or restrictions" (UN, 1975, para. 131). This second Conference of Government Experts will take place on 26 January – 24 February 1976, when more information will be given about the effects of specific weapons. On the basis of that information, the Conference will make proposals after having weighed the military advantages against the humanitarian misgivings based on the concepts of "superfluous injury", the indiscriminate effects, the laws of humanity and the demands of the public conscience.

It is self-evident that anti-personnel incendiary weapons violate many principles of the laws of armed combat. They may cause unnecessary suffering and are indiscriminate in their effects. They are inhumane and repulsive weapons contrary to "the laws of humanity and the demands of the public conscience". They should be expressly forbidden. Such an express prohibition is needed in view of the former praxis and the existing differences of opinion, apparent from national military manuals and scholarly publications. In view of the repulsive character of the weapon, the prohibition of incendiary weapons should be general, with the possible exception of some forms of anti-matériel use.

Small-calibre high-velocity weapons

As a result of military research, a new development has taken place in the field of small-calibre, for example, 5.56-mm, projectiles which facilitates a lighter weapon design and also decreases the weight of the ammunition. This enables the soldier to carry many more rounds of ammunition, given the same weight allowance. At the same time, velocity has been increased.

As a high-velocity projectile passing through tissue gives rise to strong shock waves and violent cavitation, the damage done may be extensive even if the projectile does not tumble after impact. Projectiles of high velocity and of a high length-calibre ratio are always unstable when passing through dense media such as water or human tissue. The spin is not sufficient to stabilize them under these conditions. As the projectile nearly always strikes the target at an angle to the perpendicular, it may start to tumble on impact (even though the

[12] "The government of Mexico continues to be in favour of eliminating the exception contained in subparagraph 3(b) in order that the prohibition of incendiary weapons be total." (UN, 1975, para. 139).

68

projectile does not deform on impact like a dum-dum bullet). Most of the bullet's energy will be transferred to the surrounding tissue. If the jacket of the bullet is thin, it may break under the enormous forces acting on the projectile as it tumbles, in which case the bullet will produce a true dum-dum effect although it was not primarily intended to. A typical example of hand firearms that may produce such effects is the US M16 rifle.

Projectiles with high kinetic energy which transmit a great deal of this energy to the human body usually cause severe injuries. The transmission of energy takes place in the form of a violently pulsating shock wave which breaks down tissues at a distance from the missile track itself. The shock wave destroys muscle, and parts of the skeleton can be fractured without having been in direct contact with the projectile.

As the temporary cavity pulsates, positive and negative pressure gradients alternate which give rise to a suction effect from both the entrance and the exit wound. This suction causes all high-velocity injuries to be contaminated and infected. The damaged tissue around the wound constitutes an excellent medium for bacterial growth. Infection is an important factor as regards these wounds, as it aggravates and complicates the injury. It also calls for special, resource-demanding treatment.

If the projectile strikes hard objects such as uniform buttons, bones and so on, secondary projectiles are easily formed which can give rise to serious injury far from the original missile track. If these secondary projectiles strike near the abdomen or chest, they can cause injuries which are very difficult to treat. If a high-velocity bullet strikes vital organs such as the central nervous system, the heart, major blood vessels, the liver or kidneys, death is usually instantaneous. If it hits non-vital organs, it causes severe injury which may result in permanent disability.

At the Lucerne Conference the discussion about small-calibre projectiles showed that there is no agreement on the fundamental question as to whether the new 5.56-mm bullets, which are fired at very high velocities, cause "superfluous injuries".

There was considerable criticism of the suggestion that a limit of 800 m/sec for the initial velocity of a bullet should be introduced. It was said that there was no significant increment in the severity of wounds caused by projectiles having a velocity of over 800 m/sec and that other factors, such as the shape and other characteristics of the bullet, needed to be taken into account.

All modern military rifle bullets contain an initial energy which is many times more than that required to incapacitate a man. But the amount of energy deposited in the wound depends in part upon the behaviour of the bullet in the wound. Bullets which expand, flatten, tumble or disintegrate in the wound – rather than continuing undeformed along a straight path – deposit more of the available energy in the wound.

The criticism directed at the new 5.56-mm bullets is that they tumble and disintegrate readily, thereby transferring more of the available energy to the wound. The heavier 7.62-mm bullets are more likely to perforate the body, thereby possibly taking with them as much as 80 per cent of the energy.

To the weapons designer it is more logical to design a bullet which gives up all its energy to the target. However, to deposit the greatest amount of energy while avoiding "explosive-type" wounds, the amount of energy must be reduced. This conflicts with the demand for long range, which was the original purpose of the rifle.

At the Second Session of the Diplomatic Conference, a draft proposal was introduced (CDDH/IV/201, Add. 1-3) containing the following provision:

Especially injurious small calibre projectiles.
It is prohibited to use small calibre projectiles which are so designed or have such velocity that they:
a. break or deform on or following entry into a human body, or
b. tumble significantly within the human body or
c. create shock waves which cause extensive tissue damage outside the trajectory, or
d. produce secondary projectiles within a human body.

On this point again, opinions differed widely (UN, 1975, para. 119–20) and any decisions were referred to the Third Session of the ICRC Diplomatic Conference, to take place a few months after the Second Conference of Government Experts.

Fragmentation weapons and flechettes

Fragmentation munitions act by ejecting a large number of fragments at high velocity – usually in a symmetrical pattern around the bursting munition. They can also be constructed so that the fragments are concentrated along a linear trajectory, as in certain anti-personnel mines. The size of the fragments may range from hundreds of grams down to fractions of a gram. It is possible to distinguish between two main types of fragment: those obtained by spontaneous fragmentation and those by pre-fragmentation. As regards the design of anti-personnel fragmentation munitions, there is a trend towards smaller and smaller fragments. It has been found that, at fragment velocities attainable with the newer types of explosive, even a fragment weighing a fraction of a gram may put a person out of action. Fragments from spontaneously fragmenting munitions tend to have sharp edges and irregular shapes. In the case of pre-fragmentation munitions the fragments are usually of a spherical shape for reasons dictated by aerodynamics, penetration and manufacture. The number of these pellets can be very large. (For example, each bomblet in the cluster-bomb may contain about 300 pellets, so that the whole munition can dispense about 200 000 pellets). Generally speaking, controlled fragmentation of pre-fragmentation munitions is militarily more effective than spontaneously fragmenting munitions.

Fragmentation warheads are highly effective against soft targets, such as combatants in the open or unprotected civilian populations, and vulnerable targets such as radar stations, non-armoured vehicles, light vessels, aircraft and helicopters.

Fragmentation with an impact velocity exceeding 700–800 m/sec gives rise to a "high-velocity effect" involving extensive destruction of tissues and adjacent blood vessels, nerves and other organs, and also involves a great risk of secondary fragments. Injuries caused by these effects are mostly infected. As the average size of fragments is small, they result in an increasing number of wounds which are hard to locate and fragments which are difficult to remove surgically without aggravating the damage.

In the case of warheads which detonate on impact with the ground, the unevenness of the ground results in a greater number of injuries to the head, neck and trunk than with other types of weapons. Injuries of these parts of the body incur high mortality and disability rates. One problem is the presence of fragments of material which are not visible on X-ray plates, such as plastic originating from the filler material between pre-fragmented missiles. Other materials, such as uranium and zinc, also have toxic effects.

There is also a strong possibility that the effects of these weapons (especially cluster-bombs) will be indiscriminate when they are used in large numbers in the same attack, due to the great area covered. On account of the size of the affected area, there is a great danger of hitting non-military targets even if single warheads are directed against military targets such as an anti-aircraft unit in the vicinity of a population centre.

A category of weapons which have effects similar to those described are the so-called flechettes – small metal arrows or needles. They can be used in ammunition for rifles and guns or instead of fragments in warheads. A number of warheads containing flechettes and primarily intended for attack against combatants in the open started to be developed at the beginning of the 1960s. These small darts are made of steel and usually weigh about 0.5 gram. Warheads can contain from about 2 000 up to 25 000 darts, depending on the size and calibre of the warhead to be used. Generally, the projected velocity of the darts is little higher than that of the warhead itself. A possible development of this kind of warhead is that flechettes could be made larger and have a higher projetion velocity so that they could damage light armoured vehicles, such as armoured personnel carriers. Flechette warheads are highly effective when deployed against soft targets.

From the medical point of view, flechettes obtain a "high-velocity effect" if they have an impact velocity exceeding approximately 900 m/sec, and then they often tumble rapidly after entering the human body. The kill probability of a hit by a single flechette on a human target is, however, relatively low and a number of hits on the same target are therefore necessary to gain high effects. In the latter case, multiple injuries are inflicted and these are problematic from the point of view of treatment, in addition to causing a high degree of pain and suffering. The mortality risk is high.

Fragmentation weapons have been discussed at the 1974 ICRC Conference of Government Experts. The report of the UN Secretary-General (UN, 1975, para. 121–23) clearly shows the differences in evaluation of the military effects compared with the humanitarian aspects. The general opinion was that these weapons had a specific military function, and the opinion was expressed that in this respect they could not easily be replaced by other weapons.

A draft proposal submitted to the Diplomatic Conference, was made to prohibit anti-personnel fragmentation weapons and flechettes. The pertinent provisions read

Anti-personnel fragmentation weapons
Anti-personnel cluster warheads or other devices with many bomblets which act through the ejection of a great number of small calibred fragments or pellets are prohibited for use.

Flechettes
Munitions which act through the release of a number of projectiles in the form of flechettes, needles and similar, are prohibited for use.

At the Second Session, the need was felt to have more expert information, also on the subject of fragmentation weapons and flechettes, and the decision was taken to hold a Second Conference of Government Experts in 1976. On the basis of its findings the Diplomatic Conference will decide whether these weapons should be forbidden, or whether specific use of these weapons should be prohibited.

Delayed-action weapons

This category of weapons includes land mines, booby traps and other delayed-action weapons.

Land mines are the most familiar example of time-delay weapons. They are primarily designed as counter-mobility devices, usually being implanted below the surface of the ground in patterns that restrict possible enemy movement. But anti-personnel land mines are also in wide use, and most depend on fragmentation to produce casualties. Usually, they are detonated by pressure-sensitive contact fuses, but may also be activated by vibration sensors, trip-wires or other such devices. As a rule, anti-vehicle and anti-personnel mines are used together in a minefield. Some anti-personnel mines, when triggered, pop up from the ground before exploding, thus optimizing horizontal fragmentation effects.

The various types of contact mines, that is, mines which detonate when someone comes into direct contact with them, differ greatly from other mines as regards their effects on the body. These warheads mainly injure the lower extremities and the abdominal region of a human being. The amount of high explosive in these warheads can be as low as 12–20 grams. But the detonation of this small amount of high explosive is quite sufficient to cause severe injury to a foot which detonates it. The explosive force of the somewhat larger types of land mine is quite sufficient to cause traumatic amputation. Also, there is a great risk of severe infection in injuries sustained from land mines. Mine-fields laid over large areas are likely to be indiscriminate, particularly if they are unmarked and remain active for a long time.

High explosives and certain kinds of land mines can be deployed as *booby traps*. When deployed for this purpose, the charge (mine) is fixed to some object with which the enemy's forces are expected to come into contact or pass over. A simply booby trap can be arranged without explosive charge. It may be in the form of sharp objects placed in indentations in the ground. Objects may be smeared with substances, for example excrement, which infect wounds. Booby traps are often set up on roads or paths.

It has been reported from some battle zones that booby traps consisting of explosive charges attached to the bodies of the injured or the dead have been discovered. These mainly injure medical aid personnel, who are a protected group according to international law. Therefore, such booby traps must be considered grossly inhumane and in contravention of international law as treacherous weapons. Booby traps arranged within an area where the civilian population is present or through which non-combatants may pass also have indiscriminate effects.

A draft proposal submitted to the Second Session of the Diplomatic Conference contains the following formulation: "Anti-personnel land-mines must not be laid by aircraft."

With respect to land mines in general, a Canadian proposal (CDDH/IV/202) was submitted which reads:

With the development of landmine munitions that can be emplaced remotely by such systems as aircraft, artillery or guided weapons, we are of the view that experts should consider methods of marking these minefields with some type of easily identifiable and recognized sign. This sign could be in the form of a flag or coloured pyrotechnic device that might be internationally recognized to indicate such fields. While it is appreciated that such an indication would most probably not be at the edge of such fields, a number of randomly placed markers would nonetheless be an indication of the extent of such fields.

During the Conference of Government Experts in Lucerne, the need for mines to be equipped with reliable self-destructing devices was stressed. Mention was made of the perfidious character of some booby traps, connected, for example, with the wounded or dead, so that it places the intended victim under a moral, juridical or humanitarian obligation to act in such a way as to endanger his safety.[13] Two criteria entered into the discussion on assessment of delayed-action weapons and booby traps, that is, the concept of indiscrimination and that of perfidy. Consequently the discussion turned around the question of whether one would pursue the prohibition of weapons as such or, rather, the prohibition or limitation of certain types of use of such weapons. Use of specific weapons might be allowed only under specific conditions, as for example marking the minefields.

[13] See further ICRC (1975, paras. 221 and 251–53).

It was suggested by the Chairman of the Conference that there might perhaps exist a consensus on two points: that the use of explosive devices perfidious by their very nature would be prohibited, and that there ought to be a ban on the use of booby traps representing a great danger to the civilian population (ICRC, 1975, para. 257).

The Second Conference of Government Experts will provide further information about the military and humanitarian aspects of these weapons and the methods of their use. This further information will determine whether general or specific prohibitions will be acceptable.

III. *Conclusions*

During the discussion at the Diplomatic Conference it appeared that widely divergent views existed concerning the effects of specific weapons. It may be hoped that the Second Government Experts Conference will clarify the issues. From the discussions it appeared also that in military circles there existed a certain reluctance to accept prohibitions with respect to specific weapons in general or to specific use of weapons. As Brodie (1973, p. 486) observed, the military leaders have "a great belief in the efficacy of force in dealing with recalcitrant peoples or regimes abroad". The deep-rooted conviction that power is the decisive element in the solution of conflicts has as its corollary that means of power are not easily renounced.

As in disarmament conferences, the tendency exists to oppose prohibition of weapons if one's own military apparatus has a technological lead in this respect over other weapons systems. One does not easily give away such an advantage. This amounts to a partial rationality which concentrates on the power relation at a specific moment between specific opponents. But the history of weapon development shows that it does not take long before other countries reach the same level of technological developments and obtain the same kind of weapons.

The question to be answered is whether military considerations would stand in the way of prohibiting weapons when both parties in an armed conflict have these weapons. If in such a situation the military advantages are balanced on both sides, humanitarian considerations may prevail. What is at stake here is not in the first place the prevalence of moral or humanitarian concepts, but the recognition that mankind should not be the slave of technology and should put a stop to the development of ever more sophisticated means of destruction. Ultimately, the primary issue is to prevent fighting that may put humanity itself in jeopardy. The survival issue looms behind all endeavours to prohibit repulsive and indiscriminate weapons.

The aim of the humanitarian law of warfare is to diminish the suffering in war. On this point the laws of war are more or less in competition with technology which produces ever more destructive weapons. The most crucial task of the law of armed conflicts will be to prohibit in the near future, before it is too late, the use of weapons of mass destruction, especially nuclear weapons.

References

American Chemical Society, 1973, News Service, 8 October.

The Earl of Birkenhead, 1961, *The Prof in Two Worlds. The Official Life of Professor F.A. Lindemann, Viscount Cherwell*. Collins, London.

Brodie, B., 1973, *War and Politics,* Cassell, London.

Churchill, W., 1952, *The Second World War*. Vol V, *Closing the Ring*. Cassell and Co., London.

Colloque sur l'Etat Moderne et la Croix Rouge, 11–13 September 1968. Henry Dunant Institute, Geneva.

Deutsch, K.W., 1968, *The Analysis of International Relations*. Prentice-Hall, Englewood Cliffs, N.J.

Deutsch, K.W., 1973, *Der Stand der Kriegsursachenforschung,* Paper No. 2, September 1973. Deutsche Gesellschaft für Konfliktforschung, Bonn, Bad Godesberg.

Deutsch, M., 1961, "Some Considerations Relevant to National Policy", *Journal of Social Issues,* No. 3 (Psychology and Policy in the Nuclear Age).

Falk, R.A., 1964, "The Shimoda Case: A Legal Appraisal of the Atomic Attacks upon Hiroshima and Nagasaki", *American Journal of International Law*.

Falk, R.A., 1971, *This Endangered Planet, Prospects and Proposals for Human Survival*. Random House, New York.

Fuller, J.F.C., 1961, *The Conduct of War 1789–1961*. Rutgers Univ. Press, New Brunswick.

Giovannitti, L. and Fried, F., 1965, *The Decision to Drop the Bomb*. Coward-McCann, New York.

Greenspan, M., 1959, *The Modern Law of Land Warfare*. Univ. of California Press, Berkeley.

International Committee of the Red Cross, 1949, *The Geneva Conventions of August 12, 1949*. Geneva.

International Committee of the Red Cross, 1958, *Projet de Règles limitant les Risques courus par la Population Civile en Temps de Guerre*. 2nd ed. Geneva.

International Committee of the Red Cross, 1972, *Projet de Protocole Additional aux quatre Conventions de Genève du 12 août 1949,* Article 31, Geneva.

International Committee of the Red Cross, 1973*a, Weapons that may Cause Unnecessary Suffering or Have Indiscriminate Effects*. Report on the Work of Experts. Geneva.

International Committee of the Red Cross, 1973*b, Draft Additional Protocols to the Geneva Conventions of August 12, 1949*. Geneva.

International Committee of the Red Cross, 1975, *Report on the Work of the Conference of Government Experts on The Use of Certain Conventional Weapons (Lucerne, 24.9 – 18.10 1974)*. Geneva.

International Court of Justice, 1971, *Reports of Judgments, Advisory Opinions and Orders, 21 June 1971,* Legal Consequences for States of the Continued Presence of South Africa in Namibia (South West Africa) notwithstanding Security Council Resolution 276 (1970) Advisory Opinion.

Judgment of the International Military Tribunal for the Far East, 1948, official copy. Tokyo (mimeograph).

Judgment of the International Military Tribunal for the Trial of German Major War Criminals, Nuremberg, 1946. Misc. No. 12 (1946). HMSO, London.

Kalshoven, F., 1971, *Belligerent Reprisals*. A.W. Sijthoff, Leyden.

League of Nations, 1931, *Documents of the Preparatory Commission for the Disarmament Conference (Series X): Minutes of the Sixth Session (Second Part)*.

Liddell Hart, B.H., 1960, *Deterrent or Defense. A Fresh Look at the West's Military Position*. Praeger, New York.

Materials on the Trial of Former Servicemen of the Japanese Army Charged with Manufacturing and Employing Bacteriological Weapons, 1950. Foreign Languages Publishing House, Moscow.

Melman, S., Baron, M. and Ely, D., 1968, *In the Name of America*. Turnpike Press, Annandale, Va.

Mouton, M.W., 1957, *Oorlogsmisdrijven en het Internationale Recht*. A.A.M. Stols, The Hague.

Philips, C.P., 1953, "Air Warfare and Law", *George Washington Law Review*.

Pictet, J., 1966, *The Principles of International Humanitarian Law*. ICRC, Geneva.

Pictet, J., 1969, "The Need to Restore the Laws and Customs relating to Armed Conflicts", *The Review of the International Commission of Jurists*, March.

Pruitt, D.G., and Snyder, R.C., eds., 1969, *Theory and Research on the Causes of War*, Prentice-Hall, Englewood Cliffs, N.J.

Quaroni, P., 1971, "L'Italie et la Demande de l'Angleterre", *La Revue des Deux Mondes*, July.

Röling, B.V.A., 1960, *International Law in an Expanded World*. Djambatan, Amsterdam.

Röling, B.V.A., 1961, *Recueil des Cours*, Vol. II. Académie de Droit International de la Haye.

Röling, B.V.A., 1971, *Einführung in die Wissenschaft von Krieg und Frieden*. 2nd ed. Neukirchener Verlag, Neukirchen, Vluyn.

Schelling, T.C., 1966, *Arms and Influence*. Yale Univ. Press, New Haven.

Schwarzenberger, G., 1968, *The Law of Armed Conflict*, Vol. II of *International Law as applied by International Courts and Tribunals*. Stevens & Sons Ltd., London.

Shulman, M.D., 1971, Testifying in *Hearings before the Subcommittee on Arms Control, International Law and Organization of the Committee on Foreign Relations*. US Senate 92nd Congress, First session on Arms Control Implications of Current US Defense Budget, June 16, 17 and July 13 and 14, 1971. Washington.

Sokolovskiy, V.D., 1968, *Soviet Military Strategy*, 3rd ed., Macdonald and Jane's. London.

Stockholm International Peace Research Institute, 1971*a*, *The Problem of Chemical and Biological Warfare*, Vol. I. Almqvist & Wiksell, Stockholm.

Stockholm International Peace Research Institute, 1971*b*, *The Problem of Chemical and Biological Warfare*, Vol. IV. Almqvist & Wiksell, Stockholm.

Stockholm International Peace Research Institute, 1971*c*, *The Problem of Chemical and Biological Warfare*, Vol. V. Almqvist & Wiksell, Stockholm.

Stockholm International Peace Research Institute, 1972*a*, *Resources Devoted to Military Research and Devlopment: An International Comparison*. Almqvist & Wiksell, Stockholm.

Stockholm International Peace Research Institute, 1972*b*, *The Near-Nuclear Countries and the NPT*. Almqvist & Wiksell, Stockholm.

Stockholm International Peace Research Institute, 1972*c*, *Napalm and Incendiary Weapons, Legal and Humanitarian Aspects*. Almqvist & Wiksell, Stockholm.

Stockholm International Peace Research Institute, 1973, *The Problem of Chemical and Biological Warfare*, Vol. II. Almqvist & Wiksell, Stockholm.

Stockholm International Peace Research Institute, 1974*a*, *The Problem of Chemical and Biological Warfare*, Vol. III. Almqvist & Wiksell, Stockholm.

Stockholm International Peace Research Institute, 1974*b*, *World Armaments and Disarmament, SIPRI Yearbook 1974*. Almqvist & Wiksell, Stockholm.

Stockholm International Peace Research Institute, 1974*c*, *Thermal Effects of Incendiary Weapons on the Human Body*. Almqvist & Wiksell, Stockholm (reprint).

Stockholm International Peace Research Institute, 1974*d, Tactical and Strategic Anti-submarine Warfare.* Almqvist & Wiksell, Stockholm.

Stockholm International Peace Research Institute, 1975*a, The Problem of Chemical and Biological Warfare,* Vol. VI. Almqvist & Wiksell, Stockholm.

Stockholm International Peace Research Institute, 1975*b, World Armaments and Disarmament, SIPRI Yearbook 1975.* Almqvist & Wiksell, Stockholm.

Stockholm International Peace Research Institute, 1975*c, Incendiary Weapons.* Almqvist & Wiksell, Stockholm.

Stockholm International Peace Research Institute, 1976, *Ecological Consequences of the Second Indochina War.* Almqvist & Wiksell, Stockholm.

Stone, J., 1959, *Legal Controls of International Conflict.* 2nd impr. with suppl. London.

Swedish Working Group Study, 1973, *Conventional Weapons, Their Deployment and Effects from the Humanitarian Aspect,* Recommendations for the Modernization of International Law. Stockholm (mimeograph).

Taylor, T., 1971, *Nuremberg and Vietnam. An American Tragedy.* Bantam Books, New York.

Taylor, T., 1974, "The Concept of Justice and the Laws of War", *Columbia Journal of Transnational Law,* Vol. 13.

Trials of War Criminals before the Nuremberg Military Tribunals under Control Council Law No. 10, 1950–1953, 15 volumes, Washington, Vol. XI.

Tuchman, B.W., 1967, *The Proud Tower, A Portrait of the World Before the War: 1890–1914.* Bantam Books, New York.

United Nations, *Official Records of the General Assembly,* Sixteenth Session, First Committee, 1192nd meeting, 1063rd plenary meeting.

United Nations, War Crimes Commission, 1949, *Law Reports of Trials of War Criminals.* Vol. XV, *Digest of Laws and Cases.* HMSO, London.

United Nations, 1969, *Chemical and Bacteriological (Biological) Weapons and the Effects of their Possible Use.* Report of the Secretary-General. A/7575. New York.

United Nations, 1973*a, Existing Rules of International Law Concerning the Prohibition or Restriction of Use of Specific Weapons.* Survey prepared by the Secretariat. A/9215 (Vols. I–II). New York.

United Nations, 1973*b, Napalm and other Incendiary Weapons and all Aspects of their Possible Use.* Report of the Secretary-General. A/8803/Rev. 1. New York.

United Nations, 1974, *First Session of the Diplomatic Conference on the Reaffirmation and Development of International Humanitarian Law Applicable in Armed Conflicts, Report of the Secretary-General,* 12 September 1974, A. 9669.

United Nations, 1975, *Second Session of the Diplomatic Conference on the Reaffirmation and Development of International Humanitarian Law Applicable in Armed Conflicts, Report of the Secretary-General,* 5 September 1975, A. 10195.

US War Department, 1944, *Treaties Governing Land Warfare,* War Dept. Technical Manual TM 27-251. GPO, Washington.

von Weizsäcker, C.F., 1971, *Kriegsfolgen und Kriegsverhütung.* Carl Hanser Verlag, Munich.

Wanty, E., 1968, *L'Art de la Guerre.* Tome III, De la seconde guerre mondiale à la stratégie nucléaire. Marabout, Verviers.